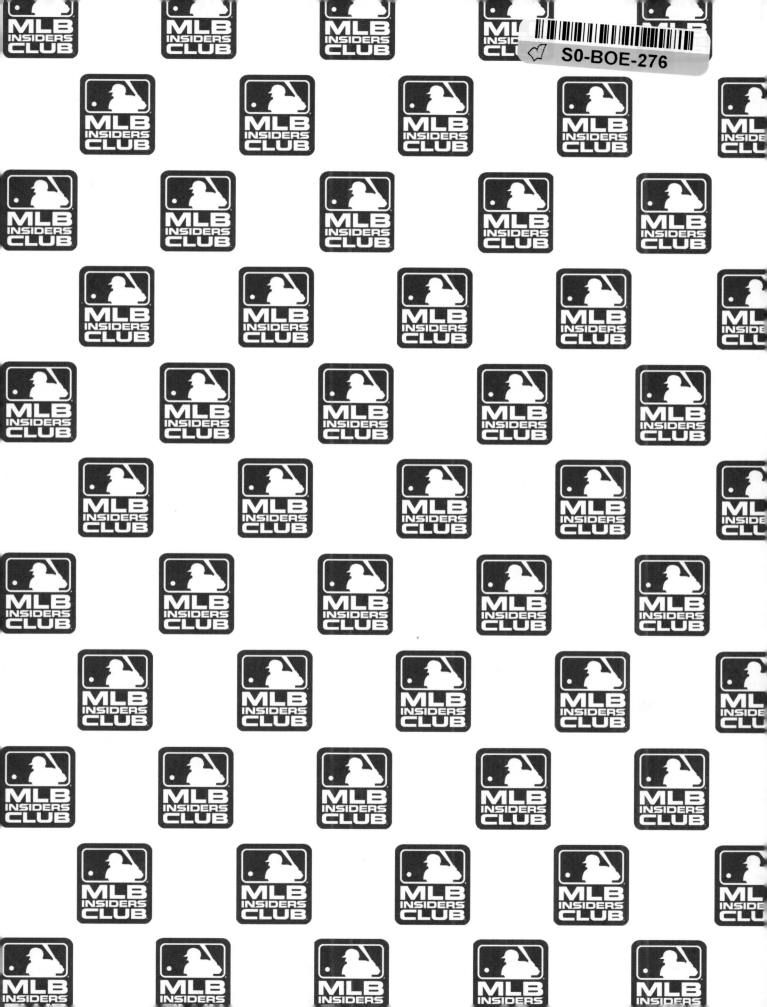

BASEBALL'S
GREATEST BALLPARKS

A tour of the most legendary venues in Major League history.

Baseball Insiders Library™

BASEBALL'S
GREATEST
BALLPARKS

A tour of the most legendary venues in Major League history.

BASEBALL'S GREATEST BALLPARKS by Steven Krasner

A tour of the most legendary venues in Major League history.

Printed in 2009

About the Author

Steven Krasner, a former Baseball MVP at Columbia University, covered the Boston Red Sox for 22 of his 33 years at The Providence (R.I.) Journal *before retiring in 2008. The author of several children's baseball books, including* Play Ball Like the Hall of Famers, *he conducts nationwide writing workshops — "Nudging the Imagination" (www.nudgingtheimagination.com) — for students and teachers.*

Acknowledgements

Major League Baseball would like to thank Pat Kelly and Milo Stewart, Jr. at the National Baseball Hall of Fame and Museum for their invaluable assistance; as well as Eric Enders, Bill Francis, Nathan Hale and Kristin Nieto for their diligent work in helping to prepare the book for publication.

Major League Baseball Properties

Vice President, Publishing
Donald S. Hintze

Editorial Director
Mike McCormick

Publications Art Director
Faith M. Rittenberg

Senior Production Manager
Claire Walsh

Associate Editor
Jon Schwartz

Associate Art Director
Melanie Finnern

Senior Publishing Coordinator
Anamika Chakrabarty

Project Assistant Editors
Chris Greenberg, Jodie Jordan

Editorial Intern
Jeremiah Sullivan

Major League Baseball Photos

Director
Rich Pilling

Photo Editor
Jessica Foster

MLB Insiders Club

Creative Director
Tom Carpenter

Managing Editor
Jen Weaverling

Prepress
Wendy Holdman

2 3 4 5 6 7 8 9 10 / 12 11 10 09

Copyright © MLB Insiders Club 2009

ISBN: 978-1-58159-411-9

MLB Insiders Club
12301 Whitewater Drive
Minnetonka, MN 55343

TABLE OF CONTENTS

INTRODUCTION 6

CHAPTER 1   IF YOU BUILD IT …
Camden Yards 8
Progressive Field 14
Coors Field 20
Rangers Ballpark in Arlington 26
Lamade Stadium, Rosenblatt Stadium 32

CHAPTER 2   THE OLD AND THE NEW, PART I
GO WEST, YOUNG MEN
Ebbets Field 34
Dodger Stadium 40
Polo Grounds 46
AT&T Park 52

CHAPTER 3   THE OLD AND THE NEW, PART II
ONE CITY, TWO PARKS
Forbes Field 58
PNC Park 64
Municipal Stadium 70
Kauffman Stadium 74
Sportsman's Park 80
Busch Stadium II 86

CHAPTER 4   OLDIES BUT GOODIES
Shibe Park 92
Comiskey Park 96
Griffith Stadium 100
South End Grounds 104
Braves Field 108
Crosley Field 112

CHAPTER 5   PUT A LID ON IT
Astrodome 116
Rogers Centre 120
Safeco Field 124
Metrodome 128

CHAPTER 6   THE HOLY HOUSES
Fenway Park 132
Wrigley Field 138
Tiger Stadium 144
Yankee Stadium 150

SOURCE NOTES/CREDITS 156

INDEX 158

INTRO

Although it's a matter of provincial dispute, the city of Hoboken, N.J. — perched just west of Manhattan — claims to have been the site of the first organized baseball game in 1846. The match was contested by two New York-based teams that took a ferry across the Hudson River to a park called Elysian Fields because it provided them the open space they did not have in New York City.

Whether or not the first game took place there, Elysian Fields was an example of the kind of pastoral spaces where the earliest contests were held. It was in such communal "ballparks" that the seeds of our national pastime were planted and where, with the care of those who gathered to watch, the game flourished.

Soon professional baseball clubs, funded by devoted fans, were fencing in their fields and erecting grandstands. Ticket-buying spectators packed wooden bleachers in the waning days of the 19th century, rooting for the local team to push a few runs across home plate. And to fans it can feel like more than a coincidence that the five-sided home plate is so named. In times of individual insecurity and international conflagration, the ballpark has been a refuge.

Trips to the stadium — whether to the Polo Grounds in New York City, Fenway Park in Boston or AT&T Park in San Francisco — have provided a sense of constancy across generations. These pilgrimages to the most hallowed places in American sport

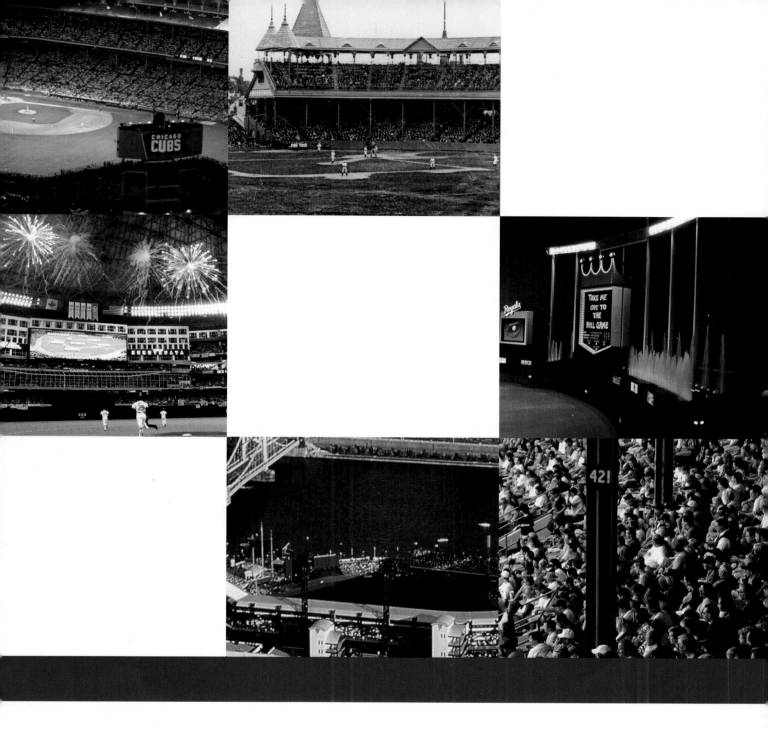

have strengthened familial bonds and forged friendships. Through the years the parks have been both strikingly similar and refreshingly diverse. The bases may always be 90 feet apart, but each club's home field has fashioned a unique atmosphere and architecture of its own, and been home to amazing plays, games and players.

If the ballparks of yesteryear had voices to relay the thrilling and record-setting events they hosted inside, then surely the tales they would tell would be the ones contained in this volume. Those voices would urge you to travel back in time to watch Connie Mack direct the A's at the French Renaissance-inspired Shibe Park in Philadelphia, to witness Mickey Mantle smash his mythic homer out of

Griffith Stadium in Washington, D.C., to take in a Negro Leagues game at Municipal Stadium in Kansas City, or to listen to Mark "The Bird" Fidrych tell the baseball not to fly out into the overhanging right-field bleachers at Detroit's Tiger Stadium.

Although such on-the-field moments are oft recounted by the public, it is often the small details that carry the most personal resonance. Whether it's the sound of Hilda Chester ringing her cowbell at Ebbets Field or the taste of a Primanti Brothers' sandwich at PNC Park, each stadium has signature elements that only a true fan could ever know about.

Come along for a tour. See and hear for yourself.

7

CHAPTER 1

IF YOU BUILD IT...

Opening Day: April 6, 1992
Dimensions: LF: 333 ft.;
LF Alley: 364 ft.; CF: 400 ft.;
RF Alley: 373 ft.; RF: 318 ft.;
Height of Fence RF/C: 25 ft.
First Pitch: Rick Sutcliffe (BAL)
First Home Run:
Paul Sorrento (CLE)
Original Capacity: 48,079
Cost: $110 Million

CAMDEN YARDS

When it came time to replace an aging Memorial Stadium in the early 1990s, the Baltimore Orioles elected to go downtown — hardly an area known for its safety in those years. Built on an 85-acre plot, Camden Yards became the Orioles' new home on April 6, 1992.

The opening of Oriole Park at Camden Yards helped revitalize the city's Inner Harbor District, a part of Baltimore that was once an industrial railroad hub. The O's also thought of their new home as a new beginning for the club.

Despite concern over the facility's hitter-friendly dimensions, the Orioles' first series at Camden Yards, and of the '92 season, proved quite low-scoring. All three games against Cleveland were shutouts, with Baltimore taking two of them. A total of just eight runs were scored in the series.

The history of Baltimore and the Orioles franchise is omnipresent throughout the stadium — from the backdrop of the B&O Warehouse in right field to the street vibe outside its gates. Camden Yards is considered one of the most magnificent stadiums in the country. Fittingly, it would be there that Cal Ripken Jr. — who was well on his way to passing Lou Gehrig's consecutive-games record when the park opened — would break the storied mark.

Camden Yards at night

THE RETRO BALLPARK ERA

When Oriole Park at Camden Yards opened in 1992, it got attention for breaking from typical stadium construction — specifically, for mirroring classic parks of the early 1900s. It was the first ballpark built in nearly 40 years with brick exteriors, and the first in 89 years with exterior arches. The red bricks and exposed-steel columns would become the standard over the next two decades, as baseball transitioned back to designing fields with asymmetrical dimensions like those at Shibe Park, Forbes Field and Fenway Park.

Oriole Park offers a panoramic view of Baltimore's skyline and right field is framed by the B&O Warehouse, which was built between 1898 and 1905. A remnant of the Baltimore & Ohio Railroad station, the warehouse is the longest building on the East Coast at 1,016 feet.

While the capacity of Camden Yards is more than 48,000, its intimacy makes the fans feel as if they are always part of the action, again harkening back to the stadiums of the early 20th century.

Camden Yards was styled after ballparks of the early 1900s, known for their intimate capacities and asymmetrical dimensions.

LONGEST HOME RUNS TO LAND ON EUTAW ST.

DISTANCE	BATTER	TEAM	DATE
443 ft.	Henry Rodriguez	MON	6/17/97
440 ft.	Mo Vaughn	BOS	7/7/96
440 ft.	Jim Thome	CLE	7/26/96
435 ft.	Ben Grieve	TB	8/20/02
431 ft.	Paul O'Neill	NYY	4/30/96
430 ft.	Lee Stevens	CAL	5/23/92
430 ft.	David Ortiz	BOS	9/9/03
430 ft.	Lance Berkman	HOU	6/18/08

BOOG'S BAR-B-Q

Beyond Camden Yards' center-field gate lies an Orioles fan's paradise. Eutaw Street runs alongside the B&O Warehouse and offers more than concessions and souvenirs, mixing in franchise history by honoring Orioles legends with statues and numbers. Bronzed baseballs are imprinted in the cement walkway to commemorate home runs hit out of the park.

One of the street's most popular spots is Boog's Bar-B-Q, a food stand run by Orioles great Boog Powell, located directly behind the center-field bleachers. Customers can choose from a menu that features hickory-smoked beef, pork and chicken — the smell of which is known to float over the concourse beyond the right-field fence and into the bleacher seats.

Powell, a mountain-sized first baseman when he played for the Orioles from 1961–74, is still a large presence in the area. The four-time All-Star regularly pulls up a chair and signs autographs as visitors enjoy their food. That is, if he has the time. Boog is often busy in the kitchen, stirring pots of baked beans.

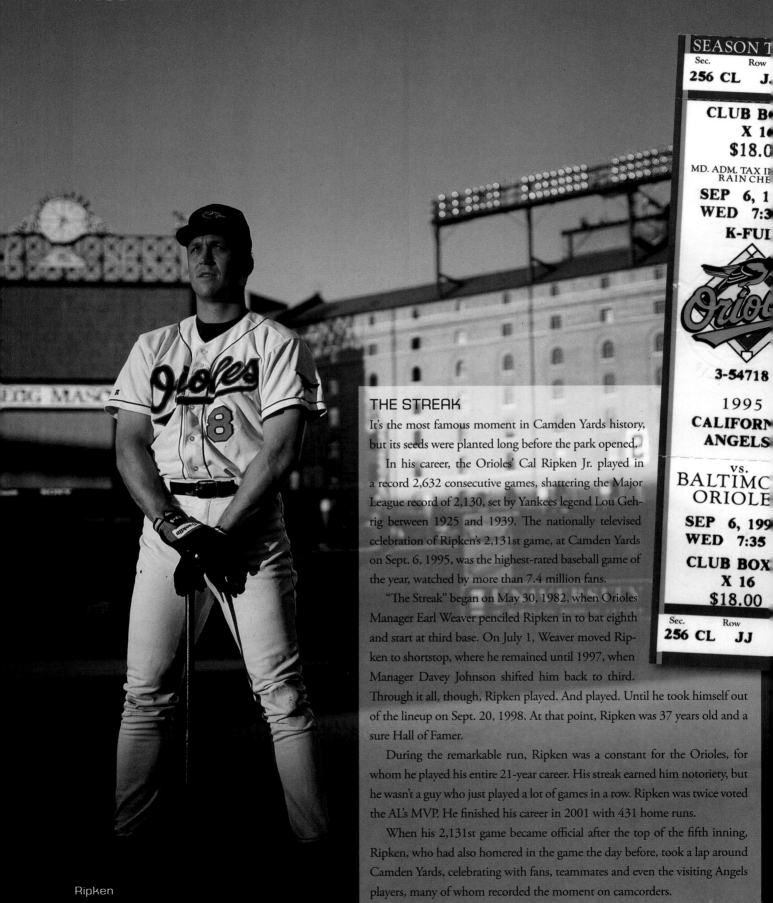

Ripken

THE STREAK

It's the most famous moment in Camden Yards history, but its seeds were planted long before the park opened.

In his career, the Orioles' Cal Ripken Jr. played in a record 2,632 consecutive games, shattering the Major League record of 2,130, set by Yankees legend Lou Gehrig between 1925 and 1939. The nationally televised celebration of Ripken's 2,131st game, at Camden Yards on Sept. 6, 1995, was the highest-rated baseball game of the year, watched by more than 7.4 million fans.

"The Streak" began on May 30, 1982, when Orioles Manager Earl Weaver penciled Ripken in to bat eighth and start at third base. On July 1, Weaver moved Ripken to shortstop, where he remained until 1997, when Manager Davey Johnson shifted him back to third. Through it all, though, Ripken played. And played. Until he took himself out of the lineup on Sept. 20, 1998. At that point, Ripken was 37 years old and a sure Hall of Famer.

During the remarkable run, Ripken was a constant for the Orioles, for whom he played his entire 21-year career. His streak earned him notoriety, but he wasn't a guy who just played a lot of games in a row. Ripken was twice voted the AL's MVP. He finished his career in 2001 with 431 home runs.

When his 2,131st game became official after the top of the fifth inning, Ripken, who had also homered in the game the day before, took a lap around Camden Yards, celebrating with fans, teammates and even the visiting Angels players, many of whom recorded the moment on camcorders.

BABE RUTH

George Herman Ruth is associated most closely with New York. But in fact, he was born in Baltimore — right down the street from Camden Yards. Ruth's father even ran a cafe that stood at the corner of Conway Street & Little Paca, located on what is now center field.

Ruth was a bit of a rowdy child, and tended to get into more than his fair share of trouble. At just 8 years old, he was sent to St. Mary's Industrial School for Boys, where he eventually learned to play baseball. By the time he was 18, Ruth was garnering attention. One of his teachers wrote to Jack Dunn, the manager of the Baltimore Orioles' minor league team.

Dunn ended up buying the youngster at $600 for six months in 1914. When Dunn brought him to the Orioles, Ruth's new teammates referred to him as Dunn's new "babe." The nickname stuck.

On April 22, 1914, Ruth pitched a shutout in his first game for the Orioles. Soon the Boston Red Sox purchased him, and Ruth was on his way to becoming a legend on and off the diamond. But his Baltimore roots are not forgotten. The Babe Ruth Museum stands just blocks from Camden Yards.

Babe Ruth Museum

IF YOU BUILD IT...

PROGRESSIVE FIELD

Ten years passed between the Cleveland Indians' initial discussions of building a new home field, and the delivery of the first pitch in a regular-season contest at that new ballpark. But in 1994, Jacobs Field, originally named after former team owners, the Jacobs brothers, was born. The ballpark has since been renamed Progressive Field.

Before they moved to the city's downtown district, the Indians played in a cavernous, 74,483-seat ballpark known as Cleveland Municipal Stadium, which the team shared with the NFL's Cleveland Browns. Nicknamed "The Mistake By The Lake" because of its dearth of creature comforts and also due to its proximity to Lake Erie, the park's lack of intimacy was noticeable for years when the Indians drew just 10,000 to 20,000 fans to games on a virtual nightly basis.

But the new stadium helped the organization to turn around its fortunes on the playing field. And in addition to aiding the team's popularity, the new ballpark played a crucial role in the revitalization of Cleveland's downtown district.

With architecture designed to reflect Cleveland's urban identity, the new stadium featured an exposed steel design, which matched the construction of bridges in the area, and vertical light towers meant to mirror the prominent image of smoke stacks and office buildings downtown.

Opening Day: April 4, 1994
Dimensions: LF: 325 ft.; LF Alley: 368 ft.; CF: 400 ft.; RF Alley: 375 ft.; RF: 325 ft.; Height of Fence RCF: 8 ft.
First Pitch: Dennis Martinez (CLE)
First Home Run: Eric Anthony (SEA)
Original Capacity: 42,865
Also Known As: Jacobs Field
Cost: $169 Million

IF YOU BUILD IT...

1995 CLEVELAND INDIANS
TEAM RECORD: 100-44 (.694)
ATTENDANCE: 2,824,745

PRIMARY LINEUP	
NAME	Position
Tony Pena	C
Paul Sorrento	1B
Carlos Baerga	2B
Jim Thome	3B
Omar Vizquel	SS
Albert Belle	LF
Kenny Lofton	CF
Manny Ramirez	RF
Eddie Murray	DH

PLAYOFF BERTHS

Maybe it was the plush surroundings of a new ballpark that inspired Cleveland, for so long an also-ran, to go on a winning spree. Maybe it was the stream of talent brought in by General Manager John Hart and managed by Mike Hargrove.

From 1960 to 1993, the Indians' final year at Cleveland Stadium, the team finished better than fourth in just one season — 1968, when it ended the year in third.

After a strike shortened the club's promising 1994 season, Cleveland built on that success in 1995, and finished first in the division by 30 games. That campaign brought home the first of six division titles, and led to two World Series appearances. Fueling the run was a group of players including Carlos Baerga, Kenny Lofton, Sandy Alomar Jr., Albert Belle, Jim Thome and Manny Ramirez. Still, Cleveland ended the decade seeking its first World title since 1948.

16

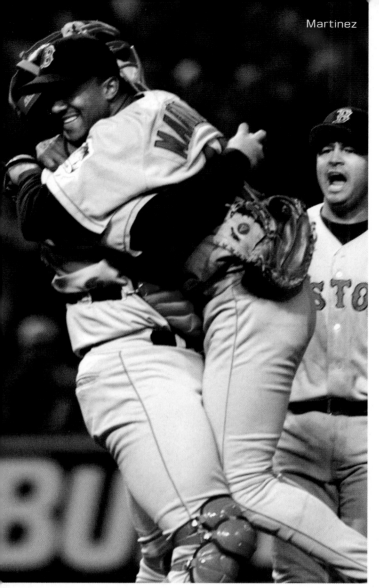

Martinez

Adams first became known for his cheering tool in 1973, when he used it during a game at Cleveland Municipal Stadium. The Indians won that day, 11-5.

A SORT-OF NO-HITTER

Pedro Martinez was hurting on Oct. 11, 1999. Battling a sore back and shoulder, he left the Jacobs Field visitors' bullpen and entered the decisive Game 5 of the ALDS against the Indians, with an ALCS berth riding on the outcome.

Martinez's Sox trailed, 8-7, when Boston's Darren Lewis doubled to lead off the top of the fourth. An Indians pitching change didn't thwart the Red Sox's rally as Lewis advanced to third on an error by second baseman Roberto Alomar and later scored to tie the game, 8-8. Martinez took the mound in the bottom of the fourth. Throwing fastballs at 95 to 96 mph when he was healthy that year, he topped out around 90 during Game 5 but still shut down the Indians' offense over the final six frames. The Dominican hurler did not allow a hit, striking out eight batters, as Boston notched a 12-8 victory and advanced to the ALCS.

THE FANS

When John Adams goes to Indians games at Progressive Field, he always brings along his bass drum.

Adams first became known for his cheering tool in 1973, when he used it during a game at Cleveland Municipal Stadium. The Indians won that day, 11-5. Adams, then 22 years old, thought that maybe he had found a good-luck charm for his oft-struggling team.

When the Indians moved into their new home in 1994, Adams and his drum moved over, too, though he needed two season tickets — one for him and one for the instrument. Adams' fandom took on a life of its own, and his persistence in rallying Cleveland fans as well as the team brought him a unique honor. In 2006, the Indians gave out collectible John Adams figurines.

Adams

IF YOU BUILD IT…

SELLOUT STREAK

The buzz that had begun to surround the Cleveland franchise shortly after the Tribe moved into its brand new ballpark got louder and louder in 1995. The youthful and talented Indians battered their opposition on a nightly basis, and zoomed to a commanding lead atop the American League Central.

With the home team up 10 games in the standings by July 2, and well on its way to the club's first AL pennant since 1954, Cleveland fans flocked to the ballpark, filling it to capacity game after game. The Indians sold out their June 12, 1995, game against Baltimore, playing in the presence of 41,845 enthusiastic spectators. Although no one was conscious of it at the time, that game was the beginning of a record-setting trend.

As the Indians developed a reputation as one of the most dynamic and successful teams in the Major Leagues, more and more fans came out to watch their team play. Cleveland sold out 455 consecutive games at its home field up until April 4, 2001. That day, a crowd of just 32,763 showed up to see the Indians host the Chicago White Sox. It was the first non-sellout since June 7, 1995 — just more than six years earlier.

The Indians had gone 2,127 days in between non-sellout contests. During the streak, Cleveland drew a total 19,324,248 fans to the Jake, as the park was then affectionately nicknamed. Shortly after setting the mark, Cleveland retired No. 455, by hanging it alongside the jersey numbers of legendary franchise greats.

The 455 consecutive sellouts were a Major League record at the time, but the number was eclipsed by the Boston Red Sox at Fenway Park on Monday, Sept. 8, 2008, in a game against Tampa Bay.

Alomar

HOMETOWN HERO

Sandy Alomar Jr. entered the 1997 season having gotten past a frustrating spell of injuries. It all seemed to be falling into place for the Indians catcher, even if he wasn't chosen to start behind the plate in the All-Star Game at his home field on July 8.

It would have been nice, but Rangers backstop Ivan Rodriguez was the fans' choice. Regardless, that night turned out to be a very special one, indeed, for the hometown catcher.

In the seventh inning, Alomar came to the plate with the score tied, 1-1, a runner at first and two outs. He connected for a two-run homer off Shawn Estes, ultimately giving the American League a 3-1 victory.

For his efforts, Alomar was named the game's MVP, making him the first player in history to receive the honor in his home ballpark. An exuberant crowd of 44,916 hailed his achievement.

IF YOU BUILD IT...

LoDo District

Opening Day: April 26, 1995
Dimensions: LF: 347 ft.; LF Alley: 390 ft.; CF: 415 ft.; RF Alley: 375 ft.; RF: 350 ft.; Height of Fence LF/CF: 8 ft.; Height of Fence RF: 14 ft.
First Pitch: Bill Swift (COL)
First Home Run: Rico Brogna (NYM)
Original Capacity: 50,200
Cost: $215 Million

COORS FIELD

No element has played a more significant role in the evolution of Coors Field than the high altitude of Denver, Colo. Aside from being accompanied by a scenic mountain view, the city's thin air has greatly affected the Rockies' history and success. While the stadium was being built, the franchise even installed a row of purple seats across the entire upper deck of Coors Field that marks the point exactly one mile above sea level.

Although the decision to build Denver's first baseball-specific stadium was approved in 1990, the Rockies played their first two seasons at Mile High Stadium, also home to the NFL's Denver Broncos. When Coors Field opened in 1995, it became another in a sequence of parks designed during the 1990s with a feel reminiscent of retro baseball stadiums.

Coors Field is located in the middle of Denver's bustling LoDo (Lower Downtown) District. The stadium was originally designed to hold 43,000 spectators. But the young Rockies' instantly impressive attendance at Mile High prompted an increase in capacity to more than 50,000.

IF YOU BUILD IT...

HOME RUNS AT COORS FIELD	
PRE-HUMIDOR	
YEAR	HOME RUNS
1995	241
1996	271
1997	245
1998	212
1999	303
2000	245
2001	268

HOME RUNS AT COORS FIELD	
POST-HUMIDOR	
YEAR	HOME RUNS
2002	232
2003	230
2004	221
2005	170
2006	168
2007	185
2008	174

HOME RUNS

When designing Coors Field, the Colorado Rockies' management expected the park to surrender home runs at a greater frequency than most other ballparks in the Majors.

Because the stadium sits one mile above sea level, a baseball travels 9 percent farther than it does at sea level. For example, a 400-foot homer in a sea-level park turns into a 440-foot shot in Denver. Therefore, players and fans alike have always kept a close eye on the offensive numbers produced at Coors Field. On occasion, even the validity of outstanding seasons by players like Rockies outfielder Larry Walker — who took home the 1997 National League MVP Award — have been greeted with a certain level of skepticism due to the hitter-friendly nature of his home ballpark.

Anticipating the issue, an attempt to even things out for pitchers was made as the park was being designed. The fences of the park, which came to be nicknamed Coors Canaveral, were pushed back farther than you would find at other stadiums. Left field sits at 347 feet, center field at 415 feet and right field at 350. The power alleys are 390 in left-center and 375 in right-center.

In spite of the effort, balls still flew out of the yard at a record pace. The home-run hysteria reached a crisis point (as far as pitchers were concerned) in 2001, when teams combined for an average of 3.31 homers at Coors Field per game — totaling 268 on the season. That equaled an astounding combined 13.40 runs per game that year when the Rockies played at home. Finally the next year, Colorado would aid the situation by installing a humidor to regulate the atmosphere's affect on their baseballs.

Nomo

INAUGURAL NO-NO

Suggesting that a no-hitter at Coors Field — the home run launching pad — was unlikely would have been taken as a statement of fact on the morning of Sept. 17, 1996. Pitchers considered it a moral victory if they held opponents to three or four runs.

So when the Dodgers' Hideo Nomo stepped onto the rubber in a game at Coors Field that day, no one expected him to author the first no-no in the ballpark's history.

But that is exactly what Nomo did, mowing down Colorado in a 9-0 win in which he walked four and struck out eight. In the 110-pitch gem, he threw 66 strikes and became the first Japanese pitcher to hurl a no-hitter in the Major Leagues.

The game started two hours late because of rain. Due to the soggy conditions, Nomo wasn't comfortable going through the gyrations of his normal wind-up on the wet pitching rubber. Starting in the fourth inning, he pitched out of the stretch, even with no one on base.

Although at first the rain may have appeared a disadvantage for Nomo — forcing him to abandon his trademark corkscrew-style delivery — Colorado was still baffled by his new look.

THE HUMIDOR

It was clear that Major League Baseball needed to come up with a remedy for the number of home runs being hit at Coors Field. It had even become difficult for the Rockies to build and maintain a strong pitching staff — let alone entice quality pitchers to play there without offering exorbitant contracts. Even a curveball was tough to throw effectively at Coors Field due to the lack of resistance on a spinning ball. Denver's thinner air caused more breaking balls to hang, making them easier to hit. In the arid climate, those hits went farther due to hardened baseballs.

In 2002, the Rockies started storing baseballs in a giant humidor — a temperature and humidity-controlled aluminum storage area — that created an atmosphere about 500 percent of the humidity standard for Denver.

The humidor was effective, and since its installation, home run numbers at Coors Field have averaged out. By 2008, records were set in Denver for fewest homers (2.15) and runs (10.26) per game since the park was built.

THE WINNING STREAK

There are hot streaks, and then there are HOT STREAKS, like the one the 2007 Rockies parlayed into their first World Series appearance in the franchise's 15-year history.

With about two weeks left in the regular season, Colorado was in fourth place in the NL West, four games above .500 and 6.5 games behind the division-leading Diamondbacks.

On that day, Sept.. 16, the Rockies crushed Florida, 13-0. The rousing win sparked an almost unheard of 21-1 surge that propelled the Rockies on an improbable trip to the World Series.

Starting with the Marlins win, Colorado won 11 straight, lost one, and took its last two regularly scheduled games, tying San Diego for the NL Wild Card. The Rockies dramatically claimed

that berth during a one-game playoff at Coors Field, winning, 9-8, in the bottom of the 13th inning.

Colorado carried the streak into the playoffs, sweeping Philadelphia in the Division Series and Arizona in the NLCS, becoming the second team ever to win its first seven games in the postseason, joining the "Big Red Machine" Cincinnati Reds of 1976.

Colorado was forced to wait eight days before the World Series, and seemingly lost its magic during the idle time. The Red Sox ultimately swept Colorado for the championship.

RANGERS BALLPARK IN ARLINGTON

After pulling up its stakes and moving west from the nation's capitol in 1972, the Rangers franchise didn't settle down into a home of its own until 1994 when Rangers Ballpark in Arlington was built. While many of the retro stadiums built in the 1990s were situated in downtown areas, the Texas Rangers veered off that path in constructing their new ballpark in Arlington, a small city between Dallas and Ft. Worth, that had housed the club's previous — and outdated — stadium.

When the venture was in the planning stages there was some thought to building a dome or a stadium with a retractable roof because of the extreme heat in the area. That notion, however, was not acted upon. Instead, an open-air ballpark was built. To compensate for the heat most games are played at night when the temperatures are lower. Much to the excitement of local fans, the Rangers' new home, which goes by the simple name of The Ballpark in Arlington, took just 23 months to construct.

A five-deck grandstand runs around the stadium, with the exception of an area of the outfield where an office complex stretches from left-center to right-center. So instead of leaving a portion of the outfield area open for a better view of the skyline, as other stadiums of the era did, Rangers Ballpark in Arlington is entirely enclosed.

Opening Day: April 11, 1994
Dimensions: LF: 334 ft.; LF Alley: 388 ft.; CF: 400 ft.; RF Alley: 388 ft.; RF: 325 ft.; Height of Fence RF/CF: 8 ft.; Height of Fence LF: 14 ft.
First Pitch: Kenny Rogers (TEX)
First Home Run: Dave Nilsson (MIL)
Original Capacity: 49,178
Cost: $191 Million

GEORGE W. BUSH

More than a decade before he was elected president of the United States, George W. Bush was a minority owner of the Texas Rangers franchise, having bought a small stake in the team in 1989. Shortly after Bush came aboard, the new ownership group announced its desire to leave Arlington Stadium, a Minor League facility that had been built in 1965 and later converted to the Rangers' home when they relocated from Washington, D.C.

The old ballpark, while it had the ability to seat 43,521, didn't have modern amenities like luxury boxes, which owners believed fans craved and which were becoming increasingly commonplace in Major League stadiums. So the new owners, helped along by Bush, lobbied the local community to approve building a new ballpark.

In 1991, the citizens of Arlington, Texas, agreed to the use of public funds for the $191 million project. The plot of land was secured, and construction commenced in April the following year. By the time the 1994 season rolled around, the Ballpark in Arlington was ready to house the Rangers.

The 270-acre complex quickly became a central entertainment destination and boosted the region's appeal, drawing local and national fans throughout the season.

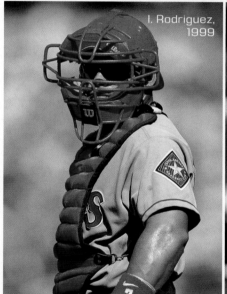

Gonzalez, 1996

Gonzalez, 1998

I. Rodriguez,
1999

A. Rodriguez, 2003

GONZALEZ'S
1,000th-HIT
GAME CAP

MOST VALUABLE PLAYERS

Rangers Ballpark in Arlington is known as a hitter-friendly stadium. So it isn't surprising that it has been the address of four American League MVP Award winners, including three in a four-year stretch.

Juan Gonzalez started the parade, winning the award in 1996 and '98. In 1996, he batted .314 and knocked in 144 runs, edging Seattle's Alex Rodriguez by three votes. Two years later, "Juan Gone" earned the hardware again.

Catcher Ivan Rodriguez was next to take advantage of the intimate park, winning the 1999 honors. Pudge batted .332 with career bests in home runs (35) and RBI (113).

In 2001, Alex Rodriguez joined the Rangers as a free agent. In 2003, he took advantage of the stadium's comforts when he batted .298 with a league-leading 47 homers. In three seasons, A-Rod smashed 156 home runs, leading the league each year.

Rogers

PERFECTION

Just a few years earlier, Kenny Rogers had been toiling out of the bullpen. But on July 28, 1994, the first season at the Rangers' new ballpark, he was given a start against the Angels. In return, he treated the home fans to a gem, throwing just the 14th perfect game in Big League history.

Rogers joined Providence's Lee Richmond and the Reds' Tom Browning as the only left-handers to achieve pitching perfection (David Wells and Randy Johnson would later join the elite club). He stifled the Angels, 4-0, in front of 46,581 fans — at the time, the largest crowd in the ballpark's brief existence.

While he didn't even walk one batter, Rogers' competitive edge almost cost him his perfecto. Refusing to give in to hitters, he went to three-ball counts on seven batters, including four in a row at one stretch, but managed to notch an out in each case.

Center fielder Rusty Greer came to Rogers' rescue in preserving the gem, with a diving backhanded catch of Rex Hudler's leadoff sinking liner in the ninth. Rogers easily retired the next two batters, needing just 98 pitches to polish off the Angels.

BORROWING TOUCHES

Rangers Ballpark in Arlington certainly evokes Texas culture, with Lone Stars and regional stone carvings throughout. But the home of the Rangers also pays homage to other storied ballparks, evidence of which can be seen inside and outside the facility.

The red brick and granite exterior is similar to that of Baltimore's Camden Yards, and the windows are arched, as they were at Chicago's Comiskey Park. Also prominent are splashes of Ebbets Field, and Yankee Stadium, circa 1973, notably a white steel frieze.

In right field, there's a short, roofed double-decker home-run porch — clearly a nod to old Tiger Stadium in Detroit. In another bow to an early 1900s stadium, the left-field fence resembles a mini-Green Monster, a la Boston's Fenway Park. Arlington's wall isn't as tall — just 10 feet compared to the 37-foot behemoth at Fenway — but it does contain a hand-operated scoreboard, just like the one at the Red Sox's home park.

IF YOU BUILD IT...

Opening Day: 1948
Dimensions: LF: 332 ft.;
LF Alley: 360 ft.; CF: 408
ft.; RF Alley: 360 ft.; RF:
332 ft.; Height of Fence
RF/LF: 8 ft.; Height of
Fence CF: 11 ft.
Also Known As: Omaha
Municipal Stadium
Largest Capacity:
23,100
Cost: $770,000

Opening Day: 1959
Dimensions: LF: 200 ft.;
CF: 200 ft.; RF: 200 ft.
Largest Capacity: 40,000

LAMADE STADIUM

Every August, hundreds of young, budding baseball stars — from all around the country and the world — descend upon South Williamsport, Pa., to participate in or watch the Little League World Series.

Lamade Stadium has the privilege of hosting the tournament's greatly anticipated championship game each year, which pits the United States champ against the international champ.

The ballpark itself is a gem, nestled below a grassy hill that serves as a seating area beyond the outfield fence. Each summer, many fans spread out blankets and bask in the Pennsylvania sun as they watch the best 11- and 12-year-olds in the world play for both fun and prestige.

Up the hill from the stadium sits another treasure — the Peter J. McGovern Little League Museum — which offers an interactive exploration of the league's roughly 80-year history.

Lamade Stadium was built in 1959 with wooden stands, which were replaced by concrete in 1968. It was expanded by 10,000 seats in 1971 and including fans on the hill, the stadium can hold 40,000.

Lights were added to the field in 1992, and the fences were moved back from 205 feet to 225 feet, as home runs started to become increasingly commonplace.

ROSENBLATT STADIUM

In 1948, Johnny Rosenblatt realized his dream of a stadium on a hill in Omaha, Neb. Minor League games were first held there in 1949, and eventually the NCAA College Division I World Series would come to the stadium. Ever since the first college game in 1950, "The Blatt" has been the place to see the best vie for a coveted NCAA title.

Various upgrades have increased capacity from 10,000 when the stadium was first built, to 23,100. The ballpark, called Omaha Municipal Stadium until it was renamed to honor Mayor Rosenblatt in 1964, is also home to the Kansas City Royals' top farm club. But it's the College World Series that brings the spotlight to Omaha every spring.

Press and luxury boxes hang over the stands behind home plate, the bleachers are aluminum complete with seat backs, and fans tend to gather on a 5,300-square-foot patio. But the most unique characteristic of the ballpark is the unbridled enthusiasm shown by the college students and fans, yearning for a national title.

A compelling sculpture called "Road To Omaha" stands at the main entrance of the stadium. Created by local artist John Lajba, it depicts three players lifting a fourth in celebration.

CHAPTER 2

THE OLD AND THE NEW, PART 1

Opening Day: April 9, 1913
Dimensions: LF: 419 ft.;
CF: 508 ft.; RF: 301 ft.
First Pitch:
Nap Rucker (BRK)
First Home Run:
Casey Stengel (BRK)
Final Game: Sept. 24, 1957
Original Capacity: 18,000
Largest Capacity: 35,000
Cost: $750,000

EBBETS FIELD

The Flatbush neighborhood of Brooklyn wasn't much to look at in 1905 when Charles Ebbets was searching for a new home for his Dodgers. But Ebbets had a vision. He began buying small parcels of land and by 1912 he had secured 1,200 pieces of real estate, enough for him to build his ballpark.

Ebbets Field was a magnificent structure when it opened on April 9, 1913. The exterior featured a brown brick facade. Upon entering, fans passed through an 80-foot-wide entrance into a rotunda, its floor made of Italian marble arranged in the image of a baseball. The area was lit by a chandelier, with arms shaped like baseball bats.

Inside, the field was asymmetrical, with a short home run porch in right field. This design survived many renovations, although a 19-foot wire screen was placed atop a concrete wall of the same height when home runs became more commonplace in the live-ball era. One billboard ad enticed the Dodgers to "Hit sign, win suit."

The fans, meanwhile, were right on top of the action. The minimal amount of foul territory ensured spectators a fantastic view of the many historical moments at Ebbets Field, such as Johnny Vander Meer's second consecutive no-hitter on June 15, 1938.

ROBINSON'S CAP

JACKIE ROBINSON

When Jackie Robinson jogged out of the home dugout at Ebbets Field on his way to first base for the top half of the first inning on April 15, 1947, he became the first African-American ballplayer to participate in a Major League game in 63 years.

After starring in four sports at UCLA, Robinson signed a Minor League contract in 1945 with the Dodgers, whose scouts noticed his success with the Kansas City Monarchs of the Negro American League. With an entire nation following his every move, Robinson went 0 for 3 in his first Big League game. He reached base on an error, though, and scored the winning run in Brooklyn's 5-3 victory, before a crowd of nearly 26,000.

Robinson won the Rookie of the Year Award in 1947 and the Most Valuable Player Award two years later. Those were just two highlights in a Hall of Fame career defined by his skills in the game and his dignity in the face of adversity on and off the field.

BOYS OF SUMMER

By the summer of 1955, "Wait 'til Next Year" had become the all-too-familiar mantra of disappointed Dodgers fans. The Brooklyn club, of course, wasn't a bad one: It had won five pennants since 1941. But the lamentations still rose up from the streets of Flatbush as the team chronically lost in the World Series. And making the 1941, '47, '49, '52 and '53 losses in the Fall Classic all the more painful for Dodgers fans was that each

HIGHLIGHTS AT EBBETS FIELD			
DATE	OPPONENT	GAME	SCORE
10/10/16	Boston Red Sox	Brooklyn Robins win Game 3 of 1916 World Series	4-3
4/15/47	Boston Braves	Jackie Robinson debuts, breaking color barrier	5-3
10/3/47	New York Yankees	Cookie Lavagetto breaks up a no-hit bid in ninth	3-2
10/2/55	New York Giants	Duke Snider's two homers help win Game 5	5-3
9/24/57	Pittsburgh Pirates	The final game at Ebbets Field	2-0

defeat had come at the hands of the hated New York Yankees.

Unbowed by such disappointment was the Dodgers' outstanding nucleus of players, including Pee Wee Reese, Jackie Robinson, Duke Snider, Roy Campanella, Gil Hodges, Don Newcombe, Carl Erskine and Clem Labine. On Oct. 4, 1955, the beloved group — immortalized by Roger Kahn in *The Boys of Summer* — finally brought a world championship to Brooklyn. To sweeten the deal, the Dodgers earned the crown by blanking the Yankees, 2-0, in a winner-take-all Game 7, thanks to a superb pitching performance by young left-hander — and New York native — Johnny Podres.

Chester (center)

Sym-Phony Band

ECCENTRIC FANS

Even if you didn't know a "bum" in Brooklyn, you knew where to find the "Bleacher Bums," the vocal fans who always sat in the same section of outfield seats at Ebbets Field.

No one embodied the fervor more than Hilda Chester, whose passion for the Dodgers was sparked as a teenager in the 1920s and flamed for 30 years. Her doctor forbade her from yelling after a heart attack in the 1930s, so she started to bring a frying pan and an iron ladle to games, banging the makeshift instrument to show her support. In the late 1930s, the Dodgers players presented her with a brass cowbell to ring during games.

Also adding to the atmosphere at Ebbets Field was the Sym-Phony Band, a group of fans who played instruments during games. One song from their repertoire was "Three Blind Mice," which they were known to play after bad calls.

Los Angeles welcomes the Dodgers

Ebbets Field is demolished in 1960

THE MOVE WEST

The Dodgers drew 1.8 million fans to Ebbets Field in 1947, Jackie Robinson's first year in the Majors. It was no small feat considering that the park's capacity was just 32,000. But such strong attendance wasn't out of character for the club's loyal fans. The Dodgers' attendance at Ebbets Field exceeded 1 million each year from 1945–57.

But Walter O'Malley, who became the franchise's owner in 1950, wanted to build a bigger ballpark — one that would seat 52,000. New York City's Building and Trades Commission, however, wasn't jumping to accommodate O'Malley. For three years the stalemate continued as Ebbets Field slowly crumbled.

With the negotiations at a standstill, O'Malley moved the team to Los Angeles for the 1958 season. For the first time since the mid-19th century, there would be no professional baseball in Kings County. Ebbets Field was demolished in 1960.

DODGER STADIUM

Almost 50 years after Charles Ebbets relocated the Dodgers from New York's New Washington Park to Flatbush, Walter O'Malley undertook an even more ambitious task — moving the franchise all the way to California. As Ebbets had done in 1905, O'Malley found a rundown neighborhood and eventually secured a 300-acre site in Chavez Ravine, just north of downtown Los Angeles.

After playing its first four seasons on the West Coast in the Los Angeles Memorial Coliseum, the team was finally able to move into Dodger Stadium for the 1962 campaign. One of the most idyllic ballpark settings in the Majors, the bowl-shaped stadium was built into the hilly landscape, providing fans a breathtaking view of the surrounding San Gabriel Mountains and the Elysian Hills through a wide opening between the decks in left and right field.

Multicolored seats — restored to their original pastel shades of yellow, orange, turquoise and sky blue after renovations in 2006 — add to the charm and the clean, fresh feel of the park.

Even though many seats, especially those in the upper decks, are relatively far away from the field, fans have always flocked to the stadium. The Dodgers were the first team to draw 3 million fans, passing that mark for the first time in 1978, and reaching it six more times before another franchise was able to reach it once.

Opening Day: April 10, 1962
Dimensions: LF: 330 ft.; LF
Alley: 380 ft.; CF: 410 ft.;
RF Alley: 380 ft.; RF: 330 ft.;
Height of Fence in LF/CF:
10 ft.; Height of Fence from
foul poles to bullpen: 3.75 ft.
First Pitch:
Johnny Podres (LAD)
First Home Run:
Wally Post (CIN)
Original Capacity: 56,000
Cost: $23 Million

Dodgers fans on the West Coast grew up listening to Scully describe virtually all of the organization's greatest moments.

VIN SCULLY

Discovered by legendary announcer Red Barber shortly after graduating from Fordham University, New York City native Vin Scully has been a member of the Dodgers family since 1950 when he stepped into the booth with Barber.

The Dodgers were playing in Ebbets Field back then, but Scully made the move West with the team and enjoyed more than 50 seasons as the "Voice of the Dodgers" in California.

Fans always enjoyed Scully's ability to transform a baseball game into a lyric poem. Over and over he conjured up clear images in his listeners' minds with a mellifluous voice, precise language and a vast knowledge of the game.

Dodgers fans on the West Coast grew up listening to Scully describe virtually all of the organization's greatest moments, including Sandy Koufax's perfect game in 1965, Orel Hershiser's record-setting scoreless streak in 1988, and even the mad dash to the NL West title led by Manny Ramirez in 2008.

Starting when he was 25 years old, Scully was the voice of the World Series on TV and radio. For his impact on the game and his dedication to the sport, Scully received the Baseball Hall of Fame's Ford C. Frick Award in 1982, which is given annually to a broadcaster for "major contributions to baseball." He was also named Broadcaster of the Century by the American Sportscasters Association in 2000.

SANDY KOUFAX

Although they later called him the "Man With the Golden Arm," Sandy Koufax was wild early in his career. Born in Brooklyn, Koufax broke into the Big Leagues with his hometown Dodgers at the age of 19 in the mid-'50s. The left-hander conquered his control issues as he gained experience. Mixing a curveball into his repertoire, Koufax embarked on arguably the most dominant stretch ever for a pitcher. He authored four no-hitters between 1962 and 1965, including a perfect game against the Chicago Cubs on Sept. 9, 1965. The southpaw struck out a Major League-record 382 batters in 1965. From 1962–66, Koufax was virtually unbeatable. He led the NL in earned-run average each season during that stretch and won the Cy Young Award in 1963, '65 and '66, when pitchers from both leagues competed for just one award.

Koufax and teammate Don Drysdale pitched the Dodgers to World Series titles in 1963 and '65.

A private man, Koufax reluctantly made headlines due to his religious beliefs in 1965. Game 1 of that year's World Series fell on the Jewish holiday of Yom Kippur. Koufax chose to respect the holiday by not pitching the Series opener against the Twins. He did, however, pitch shutouts in Games 5 and 7 to win Series MVP honors as the Dodgers claimed the crown.

Unfortunately, Koufax had to retire after the 1966 season because of arthritis in his pitching elbow. He was just 30 years old. His career record was 165-87 with a 2.76 ERA and 2,396 strikeouts in 2,324.1 innings.

SANDY KOUFAX FROM 1962 TO 1966					
W-L	ERA	SO	IP	CG	WHIP
111-34	1.94	1,444	1,377	100	0.926

HOBBLE-OFF HOMER

Kirk Gibson had carried his potent club to the playoffs, batting .290 with 25 homers and 76 RBI during the regular season in 1988, numbers that would earn him the NL MVP Award. But bothered by hamstring and knee problems, he wasn't in the Dodgers' lineup as the World Series opened at Dodger Stadium.

On Oct. 15, Gibson was a spectator as the Oakland Athletics took a 4-3 lead into the ninth inning in Game 1. Oakland sent

Dennis Eckersley, who had locked down 45 saves during the '88 campaign, out to finish off the win. Eckersley retired the first two batters, but then he walked pinch-hitter Mike Davis.

Dodgers Manager Tommy Lasorda planned on sending Dave Anderson up to bat for pitcher Alejandro Pena. But Gibson had already grabbed a bat. He wanted to hit. A roar went up from the crowd as Gibson limped to the plate. After running the count to

Gibson

Valenzuela

FERNANDOMANIA

At first glance, Dodgers fans didn't know what to make of the portly Mexican left-hander with an unorthodox pitching motion. When he was called up in September 1980, Fernando Valenzuela, a 19-year-old rookie, would pivot on the rubber, almost turning his back to the hitter. As he did, he would look up at the sky, taking his eyes off the target.

Thanks in part to his devastating screwball — known as the "Fernando Fadeaway" — Valenzuela was back on the Big League roster for Spring Training in 1981. He tossed a shutout on Opening Day and by mid-May he was 8-0. It wasn't long before large crowds were flocking to Dodger Stadium to watch him pitch. As a result, the Dodgers' radio expanded from three outlets to 17 in Mexico as Valenzuela enjoyed unparalleled early success on the mound.

The fervor surrounding the pitching phenom even had a name — "Fernandomania." When the Dodgers went on the road, there were so many media requests to interview Valenzuela that a separate press conference had to be held in each city.

Valenzuela, amazingly, remained calm despite the frenzy surrounding him. He was poised on the mound, too, becoming the first player to win the Rookie of the Year and the Cy Young Award in the same season, which he did in 1981.

3-and-2 on Gibson, the A's relief ace threw a backdoor slider. And Gibson hooked the ball into the right-field seats for a game-winning two-run homer.

Radio announcer Jack Buck yelled, "I don't believe what I just saw!" as Gibson slowly made his way around the bases. The "hobble-off" homer was Gibson's only at-bat of the Series, and it propelled the Dodgers to a sweep of the favored Athletics.

POLO GROUNDS

Not even a fiery inferno could prevent the New York Giants from returning to 157th St. and Eighth Ave. in Upper Manhattan. When the wooden stadium — a third incarnation of the playing field known as the Polo Grounds — burned to the ground on April 14, 1911, the franchise immediately set to work on building a new home for the team.

Only two-and-a-half months later, on June 28, the Giants were back at a new wooden Polo Grounds, before a permanent structure was erected that off-season. The concrete edition of the stadium had an Italian marble facade and iron scrollwork on the seats, but it became known for its unusual oval bathtub-like shape and short distances down the left-field and right-field lines.

The distances to the outfield corners were far cozier than to the outrageously deep center field. It was just 279 feet to left and 256 feet to right. It was much more difficult to hit the ball out of the park anywhere else, though, with fences 450 feet away in left-center and right-center fields, and about 480 feet to dead center, backed by a 60-foot-high wall.

It was quite clear that Giants slugger Mel Ott appreciated the dimensions in right field, knocking 135 more home runs at the Polo Grounds than he did on the road. It helped him to become the first player in National League history to hit 500 homers.

Opening Day: April 19, 1890 (PG III); June 28, 1911 (PG IV)
Dimensions: LF: 277 ft.; LF Alley: 455 ft.; CF: 433 ft.; RF Alley: 449 ft.; RF: 258 ft.
First Pitch: Christy Mathewson (NYG)
First Home Run: Larry Doyle (NYG)
Also Known As: Brush Stadium
Original Capacity: 34,000
Largest Capacity: 56,000
Cost: $100,000

Thomson

THE SHOT HEARD 'ROUND THE WORLD

The 1951 Giants had been playing catch-up all season. They were 13 games behind the National League-leading Brooklyn Dodgers in the standings on Aug. 11, but finished the campaign on a red-hot 39-8 tear to force a three-game playoff for the NL pennant. After splitting the first two games, the Giants were trailing, 4-1, in the bottom of the ninth inning in the decisive contest.

Even on the brink of a season-ending loss, the Giants refused to go quietly. They scratched a run off tiring Dodgers pitcher Don Newcombe before he was lifted by Manager Charlie Dressen. The Dodgers skipper then summoned right-hander Ralph Branca to face Bobby Thomson with the Dodgers on top, 4-2, and runners at second and third. The Giants were two outs from defeat.

Thomson watched an arrow-straight fastball pass by him for a strike. Branca then tried a fastball up and in, hoping to set up the next pitch, which would have been a breaking ball down and away to Thomson, a right-handed hitter.

Thomson, though, made certain that the breaking ball wouldn't be needed. He took a full cut at the fastball and lofted a fly ball to left field that, thanks to the friendly dimensions of the Polo Grounds, sailed over the fence for a three-run pennant-winning homer, prompting excited Giants radio announcer Russ Hodges to exclaim: "The Giants win the pennant! The Giants win the pennant!"

MERKLE'S MISTAKE

The odd course of events began on Sept. 23, 1908, when the Chicago Cubs and the New York Giants were tied, 1-1, heading into the bottom of the ninth at the Polo Grounds. Fred Merkle went to bat with a man at first and two outs. He smacked a single, moving the runner. And when Al Bridwell followed with an RBI hit, it looked like the Giants had won, 2-1. As was the custom, Merkle and his teammates raced to the clubhouse in center field once the game ended to avoid the fans, who exited through gates in the outfield.

A rule, then rarely enforced, mandates that runners in such an event tag the next base, which Merkle had not done. Cubs second baseman Johnny Evers, cleverly looking to exploit the rule, got the ball, alerted umpire Hank O'Day and stepped on second. By then most players were gone. That night, O'Day called Merkle out, and NL President Henry Pulliam ruled the game a tie to be replayed if necessary.

RULE 56, SECTION 11 If, when the batsman becomes a base runner, the first base, or the first and second bases, or the first, second and third bases be occupied, any base runner so occupying a base shall cease to be entitled to hold it, and may be put out at the next base in the same manner as in running to first base, or by being touched with the ball in the hands of a fielder at any time before any base runner following him in the batting order be put out, unless the umpire should decide the hit of the batsman to be an infield fly.

As fate would have it, the two teams were tied atop the standings at the end of season, meaning the "Merkle" replay would decide the pennant. The Cubs won, 4-2, and Merkle's name would forever be associated with the mishap.

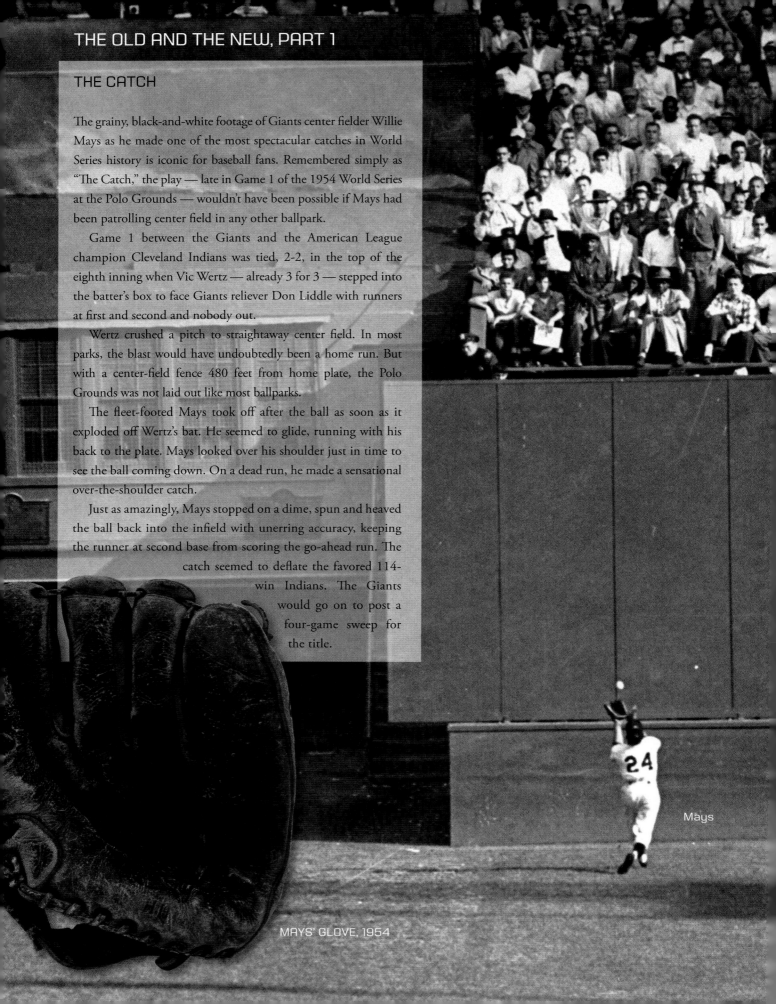

THE CATCH

The grainy, black-and-white footage of Giants center fielder Willie Mays as he made one of the most spectacular catches in World Series history is iconic for baseball fans. Remembered simply as "The Catch," the play — late in Game 1 of the 1954 World Series at the Polo Grounds — wouldn't have been possible if Mays had been patrolling center field in any other ballpark.

Game 1 between the Giants and the American League champion Cleveland Indians was tied, 2-2, in the top of the eighth inning when Vic Wertz — already 3 for 3 — stepped into the batter's box to face Giants reliever Don Liddle with runners at first and second and nobody out.

Wertz crushed a pitch to straightaway center field. In most parks, the blast would have undoubtedly been a home run. But with a center-field fence 480 feet from home plate, the Polo Grounds was not laid out like most ballparks.

The fleet-footed Mays took off after the ball as soon as it exploded off Wertz's bat. He seemed to glide, running with his back to the plate. Mays looked over his shoulder just in time to see the ball coming down. On a dead run, he made a sensational over-the-shoulder catch.

Just as amazingly, Mays stopped on a dime, spun and heaved the ball back into the infield with unerring accuracy, keeping the runner at second base from scoring the go-ahead run. The catch seemed to deflate the favored 114-win Indians. The Giants would go on to post a four-game sweep for the title.

Mays

MAYS' GLOVE, 1954

THE HOUSE THAT RUTH RENTED

Baseball fans young and old know all about The House That Ruth Built and the Bambino's historic feats in the Bronx. But most fans forget that Ruth first made his name as a one-of-a-kind slugger in a house across the Harlem River, the Polo Grounds.

When the Yankees acquired Ruth from the Red Sox before the 1920 season, they were still sharing the Polo Grounds with the Giants. A left-handed pull hitter with an uppercut swing, Ruth found the cozy 258-foot distance from the plate down the right-field line to his liking and blossomed as a powerful slugger. He finished the 1920 season with 54 longballs, an unheard-of number in an era when the offensive emphasis was on speed and guile.

Indeed, Ruth, who batted .376 and drove in 137 runs for the season, had more home runs by himself that year than all but one *team* in the Major Leagues. The following season, Ruth hammered 59 homers, drove in 171 runs and batted .378. He amassed a record 457 total bases in 152 games.

Ruth was limited to 110 games in 1922, but was still able to club 35 homers and knock in 99 runs, posting a .315 batting average in the Yankees' final season at the Polo Grounds.

The next year, the team moved to Yankee Stadium, which featured a Polo Grounds-like short distance down the right-field line for their star.

51

AT&T PARK

Visiting teams dreaded playing games at Candlestick Park in San Francisco. The wind off the bay whipped through the stadium, chilling ballplayers to the bone and wreaking havoc on any airborne baseball. Such a home-field advantage would have been a fine thing for the Giants except for the fact that they, too, were subject to the harsh conditions. Finally, after years of planning, the Giants moved into a downtown ballpark in 2000. AT&T Park, as it became known in 2006, is one of the most picturesque facilities built in the modern era.

The brick facade is highlighted by two 122-foot King Street clock towers, each topped by a 45-foot flagpole. There is also a sidewalk outside the ballpark, beyond the right-field wall, that commemorates memorable moments in the club's storied history.

Passing a statue of Giants Hall of Famer Willie Mays at the ballpark's main entrance, fans follow an indoor walkway that circles the entire park. A picturesque view from the walkway reveals the China Basin area in the Bay beyond the outfield walls, as well as the world's largest baseball glove in left-center, as the scents of garlic fries and crab cake sandwiches fill the air.

And one doesn't even need a ticket to enjoy the action during a Giants game at AT&T Park; a screen fence on the right-field wall allows passersby a free view of the field of play.

Opening Day: April 11, 2000
Dimensions: LF: 339 ft.; LF Alley: 404 ft.; CF: 399 ft.; RF Alley: 421 ft.; RF: 309 ft.
First Pitch: Kirk Rueter (SFG)
First Home Run: Kevin Elster (LAD)
Also Known As: Pac Bell Park, SBC Park
Original Capacity: 40,930
Cost: $357 Million

"SPLASH" HITS

It's high, it's far, it's — wet! It's not uncommon for the crack of the bat to be quickly followed by a splash at AT&T Park. Such titanic blasts are called "splash" hits.

While the right-field wall is just 309 feet down the line, it's 25 feet high in that area, and there's a pedestrian concourse that a ball has to clear before it can reach the water. But in the first nine seasons of baseball at AT&T Park, 65 homers cleared the fence and plopped into McCovey Cove. Career home run leader Barry Bonds knocked the first "splash" home run, launching a drive off Mets middle reliever Rich Rodriguez on May 1, 2000. Of the first 33 "splash" homers racked up by the Giants, Bonds boasted 29. He ended his Giants career with 35 of the then-total 47 bashed by the home team.

A storm of "splash" home runs was expected during the Home Run Derby portion of the 2007 All-Star Game festivities, but the event's participants found it wasn't as easy as it looked. There were three left-handed hitters in the competition, but the southpaws couldn't turn the trick. Only left-handed Milwaukee Brewers first baseman Prince Fielder was able to hit a ball into the water — but even that was foul. Fielder, though, did later hit one into McCovey Cove during a regular-season game on July 19, 2008.

McCOVEY COVE

Some people like to watch a baseball game from the bleacher seats. Others prefer the luxury of private boxes. For some fans in San Francisco, though, there is no better place to be at AT&T Park than floating around in the water.

The adventurous fans can be found beyond the right-field fence, hoping for a home run to clear the wall and sail into what is popularly called McCovey Cove, named for Giants

McCOVEY COVE HOME RUNS BY SAN FRANCISCO GIANTS	
YEAR	SPLASH HOME RUNS
2000	6
2001	11
2002	6
2003	8
2004	6
2005	3
2006	1
2007	4
2008	2

Hall of Fame first baseman Willie McCovey, who bashed 521 home runs in his 22-year Hall of Fame career. The body of water now paying homage to the slugger is also known as China Basin. Across the water from the stadium, fans can find a statue of McCovey.

Floating fans in kayaks or small boats are often armed with nets in the hope of fishing a soggy souvenir out of the water.

So while some people choose to line up at the ticket windows to purchase a seat for a game, there are other fans seeking out the various boat rental businesses on San Francisco Bay in search of a suitable vessel for a pleasant few hours on the water.

2002 WORLD SERIES

It had been 40 years since the Giants won a World Series game in San Francisco when Game 3 of the 2002 Fall Classic got underway on Oct. 22. The Giants fell to the AL champion Angels that night, doing nothing to vanquish memories of the harrowing Game 7 loss to the New York Yankees in the 1962 World Series or the sweep at the hands of the Oakland A's in the earthquake-marred 1989 Fall Classic.

On the next two evenings, though, the Giants gave their home fans plenty to cheer for, winning Games 4 and 5 of the Classic to take a 3-games-to-2 lead. Trailing 3-1 entering the bottom of the fifth in Game 4, the Giants rallied for a 4-3 victory. The next night, the 95-win San Francisco club flexed its muscles, hanging 16 runs on the Angels in a victory at then-Pac Bell Park. Unfortunately for Bay Area fans, the Giants faltered without their home crowd backing them in Anaheim. After a sixth-inning longball from Barry Bonds gave the Giants a 4-0 edge in Game 6, the Angels stormed back to win that contest as well as a dramatic Game 7.

Ichiro sent a shot toward right-center field and didn't stop running until he touched home plate, scoring the first inside-the-park home run in All-Star Game history.

Ichiro

2007 ALL-STAR GAME

When AT&T Park was built, the architects purposefully included some nooks and crannies in the outfield. And Seattle's All-Star outfielder Ichiro Suzuki found one during the 2007 Midsummer Classic. He sent a shot toward right-center field that smacked off the wall and caromed at an odd angle toward center field. The speedy Ichiro kept on running while the National League outfielders scrambled to try to track down the rolling baseball.

Ichiro didn't stop running until he touched home plate, scoring the first inside-the-park home run in All-Star Game history. The two-run shot in the fifth inning helped the American League beat the National League, 5-4. Although Ichiro, who had three hits, was named the game's Most Valuable Player, the award really could have been given to the host ballpark.

HOME RUN KING

It was only a matter of time. And health. Barry Bonds entered the 2007 season with 734 home runs, leaving him 21 shy of Hank Aaron's total of 755, which had stood as one of baseball's most revered records since 1976.

Although injuries slowed the 43-year-old's pace, Bonds moved closer to the mark as the season went along. And when he stepped into the box against Washington Nationals hurler Mike Bacsik on Aug. 7, 2007, he was tied with Aaron. The count ran full in the fifth-inning at-bat. Bacsik tried to sneak an 84-mph pitch by Bonds. He was unsuccessful.

Bonds sent the ball into the seats in right-center field, knowing as the ball left the bat, that he had passed Aaron. He threw both arms in the air in celebration and relief.

Bonds was the new holder of the career home run record, which had belonged to Aaron for 12,175 days, ever since his 715th homer on April 8, 1974, moved him past Babe Ruth. A seven-time National League MVP, Bonds added six more homers before the year was out, boosting his total to 762 in his 22 seasons in the Big Leagues.

Bonds

CHAPTER 3
THE OLD AND THE NEW, PART II

FORBES FIELD

After joining the American Association in 1882, the Pittsburg Alleghenies built a stadium, Exposition Park, where the Allegheny and Monongahela Rivers flow together to form the Ohio River. This would later be the site of Three Rivers Stadium and PNC Park.

Due to repeated flooding at Exposition Park and two instances of the stadium's roof being ripped off by fierce wind, Owner Barney Dreyfuss decided the club needed a new park. Ground was broken for Forbes Field on March 1, 1909, and Dreyfuss moved the Pirates from Exposition Park to a seven-acre site near the University of Pittsburgh, three miles from downtown Pittsburgh.

Forbes Field was one of the first parks constructed with steel and concrete. And because of the relatively cheap price of land outside of the city center at the time, the franchise was able to offer amenities to fans that other Big League clubs couldn't afford at the time, like luxury boxes and an elevator.

The stadium served as the home of the Pittsburgh Pirates through the middle of the 1970 season. It hosted the first live radio broadcast of a Big League game and great moments from Pirates stars like Ralph Kiner and Roberto Clemente.

Opening Day: June 30, 1909
Dimensions: LF: 306 ft.;
CF: 417 ft.; RF: 359 ft.; Height
of LF/CF fence: 12 ft.; Height
of RF fence: 9.5 ft.
First Pitch: Vic Willis (PIT)
First Home Run:
Mike Mitchell (CIN)
Original Capacity: 23,000
Largest Capacity: 41,000
Cost: $1 Million

CHANGING DIMENSIONS

Forbes Field was one of the first ballparks to boast a three-tiered grandstand, which ran from behind first base all the way to third base. It was also one of the first parks to feature luxury boxes, which were positioned on the third grandstand level.

The size of the new park prompted builders to provide fans with a ramp to get to their seats as well as an elevator to take visitors to the third deck. Both features were firsts for a Major League venue.

The dimensions of the playing field were spacious during the beginning of the park's existence — 360 feet to left, 409 feet to center and 376 to right. Because of the vast expanses in the outfield, triples and inside-the-park home runs were more common than at most other fields, and the residents of Forbes Field led the NL in triples in 1911 and 1912, and most years thereafter.

Like many ballparks, Forbes Field evolved along with the franchise that it housed. In 1947, the Pirates acquired power hitter

Hank Greenberg and made the decision to pull the left-field fence in from 365 to 335 feet down the line to take advantage of his powerful stroke. That change also involved the addition of a 30-by-200-foot bullpen in the area, cutting the power alley in left-center from 406 to 355 feet.

But Greenberg wasn't the only beneficiary of the construction that occurred upon his arrival. Ralph Kiner, in his second season with Pittsburgh, exploded for 51 homers, tying for the league lead. Kiner's home runs kept on coming after Greenberg retired — 40 in 1948; 54 in 1949; 47 in 1950; 42 in 1951 and 37 in 1952.

The Pittsburgh left fielder won seven consecutive home run crowns even though the Pirates struggled in the standings. In spite of the team's poor records, attendance blossomed at Forbes Field in part because fans showed up hoping to see Kiner knock one out to left field, an area that came to be called Kiner's Korner.

RALPH KINER CAREER PIRATES STATS: 1946-1953														
G	AB	R	H	2B	3B	HR	RBI	SB	CS	BB	SO	BA	OBP	SLG
1,095	3,913	754	1,097	153	32	301	801	19	1	795	546	.280	.405	.567

Cobb

1909 WORLD SERIES

The 1909 Fall Classic was a showdown between Pittsburgh's Honus Wagner and Detroit outfielder Ty Cobb.

The Pirates had a regular-season record of 110-42, and the team's star shortstop batted .339 with 100 RBI and 10 triples on the year. But Detroit, which had won 98 games, wasn't about to go down without a fight. Cobb was fresh off his third consecutive AL batting title — having hit .377 that year — and had collected 107 RBI.

Babe Adams threw a six-hitter for Pittsburgh at Forbes Field in Game 1, but Cobb turned the tables in Game 2, stealing home during a Tigers rally in a 7-2 win. Game 3 was Wagner's show; he went 3 for 5 with three stolen bases in an 8-6 Pirates win.

Wagner batted .333 (8 for 24) with six RBI and six stolen bases during the Series. Cobb did not prove as successful as his Tigers fell to the Pirates. He went 0 for 4 in Game 7 and batted a mere .231 (6 for 26) in what would be his last Fall Classic.

BABE RUTH'S LAST HURRAH

By the time legendary slugger Babe Ruth was back in the city where he got his start, playing for the Boston Braves in 1935, his skills had significantly eroded. As the team's vice president and assistant manager that year, Ruth played in just 28 games, grossing 72 at-bats. He still occasionally hit home runs, but they weren't struck with the same force as they had been during his younger days. After averaging more than 45 longballs in each campaign from 1926 to 1935, his numbers dwindled to 34, 22 and six from 1933 to his last season in 1935.

But he was still the Babe, so anything less than his former glory was a disappointment to the flocks of fans that came out to see him. It was at Forbes Field that the Sultan of Swat treated fans to one final home run show on May 25, 1935. Not surprisingly, the larger-than-life baseball hero went out with a bang. Three of them, in fact.

Ruth began the game with a two-run home run in the first inning, and he crushed another two-run bomb in the third. After singling home a run in the fifth, Ruth came up to the plate again in the seventh with a runner on base. He launched a long fly ball to right field that not only cleared the fence, but also soared over the double-deck grandstand, which stood 86 feet high and was measured at more than 300 feet from home plate. The ball came to rest on the roof of a house across the way, on Bouquet Street. It was the first home run ever to clear the right-field roof of Forbes Field.

That was longball No. 714 for Babe Ruth, the final blast of his Hall of Fame career. Arguably the most renowned player in the history of the game, he retired just five days later.

MAZEROSKI'S SERIES-WINNING HOMER

Pirates second baseman Bill Mazeroski thought that Game 7 of the 1960 World Series was in the bag after teammate Hal Smith hit a homer in the bottom of the eighth to give Pittsburgh a 9-7 lead. But the New York Yankees rallied for two runs in the top of the ninth, tying the game. Mazeroski, leading off the bottom of that inning, found himself in a pressure-packed situation. He grabbed his bat and walked up to the plate, prepared to dig in against Yankees right-hander Ralph Terry.

The first pitch was high. Yankees catcher Johnny Blanchard yelled to Terry to get the ball down. Terry did just that. His next pitch was low. And Mazeroski smacked it to left field.

Yankees left fielder Yogi Berra drifted back to the high, ivy-covered brick wall. But the ball flew out of Forbes Field, hitting a tree beyond the fence and sending the home crowd of 36,683 into a state of delirium, as they celebrated Mazeroski's homer and the Pirates' World Series title.

Mazeroski, meanwhile, was racing around the bases, the hero of the World Series. Known for his defensive skills, he was by no means an outstanding hitter. But on Oct. 13, 1960, Mazeroski became the first player to hit a home run to end a World Series.

PNC PARK

After decades of playing in the cavernous setting of Forbes Field, which were followed by 30 seasons at the "cookie-cutter" Three Rivers Stadium, the Pittsburgh Pirates decided that bigger wasn't necessarily better. In April 1999, the team broke ground on PNC Park.

The franchise built the stadium on the site of its first home, Exposition Park, along the Allegheny River. The field, which opened on March 31, 2001, is the second-smallest stadium in the Majors. Its 38,496 capacity is greater than just Fenway Park's 37,400 (considering that some teams block off certain seats in their ballparks, creating artificially low listed capacities). PNC provides a more intimate experience than its much larger predecessors, but it does have a number of characteristics that are similar to Forbes Field, including a brick exterior and masonry arches.

Still, PNC Park has several signature elements of its own. Most notably the park provides an outstanding view of the downtown Pittsburgh skyline. In addition, the Pirates franchise has paid homage to its long and storied history by featuring statues of several of its greatest all-time players, as well as in deciding the height of the right-field fence. The wall was built to stand 21 feet tall, in honor of Hall of Fame right fielder Roberto Clemente, who wore uniform No. 21.

Opening Day: April 9, 2001
Dimensions: LF: 325 ft.; LF Alley: 386 ft.; Deep LCF: 410 ft.; CF: 399 ft.; RF Alley: 375 ft.; RF: 320 ft.
First Pitch: Todd Ritchie (PIT)
First Home Run: Sean Casey (CIN)
Original Capacity: 38,365
Cost: $216 Million

C PARK
HOME OF
THE PITTSBURGH PIRATES
HOME PLATE
J.P. "HONUS"
WAGNER

THE ALLEGHENY RIVER

The Allegheny River runs beyond the boundary of PNC Park, behind the right-field seats. When the stadium opened in 2001, Pirates officials were hoping to generate publicity from what they called "splashdown" homers — balls that would leave the park and touch down in the Allegheny behind the right-field seats. The team even had a sponsored sign prepared inside the park to keep track of each shot.

After the conclusion of the first season at PNC Park, however, the number of "splashdown" longballs was still sitting at zero. Over the course of the entire season, no one who played for the Pirates, or any other team for that matter, had been able to launch a home run into the Allegheny River — a drive that would have had to travel a minimum of 456 feet to reach the water on the fly. The sponsored sign was changed before the second season at PNC Park to instead show the total number of overall Pirates homers.

But on July 6, 2002, Houston Astros left fielder Daryle Ward crushed a fifth-inning grand slam off Kip Wells that sailed over the right-field fence, cleared the concrete wall at the riverbank, and dropped into the Allegheny River. The home run was measured at 479 feet, and it came in the 127th game played at PNC Park.

SAME SITE, DIFFERENT PARK

PNC Park sits nearly on top of the site of Exposition Park — home of Pittsburgh's franchise through the days of the Players League, the American Association, the National League and the Federal League.

Situated on the flood-prone north bank of the Allegheny River, as PNC Park is now, Exposition Park offered a similar view of downtown Pittsburgh. The ballpark — which featured

a single grandstand that, much like Forbes Field, stretched from first base to third base — was the site of the first-ever World Series in 1903. The Pirates won the fourth game of that Series at Exposition Park and took a 3-games-to-1 lead. But they dropped the next two contests at home and wound up unable to claim the world championship. The Pirates fell to Boston, 5 games to 3, in the Series — a best-of-nine event at the time.

Exposition Park was also the Pirates' home during the glory days of superstar Honus Wagner, who joined the club in 1900. Wagner won eight batting titles, hitting over .300 in 16 seasons. He finished with a career batting average of .327 and was one of five members in the inaugural class to enter the Hall of Fame in 1936.

The Pirates' last game at Exposition Park took place on June 29, 1909. The next day, the team moved into Forbes Field.

The Primanti sandwich became the Steel City's signature culinary treat.

LOCAL CUISINE

Joe Primanti and his nephew, John, first served sandwiches from a wooden lunch stand in Pittsburgh's Strip District during the Great Depression. In the years that followed, the Primanti sandwich — grilled meat, cheese, tomatoes, cole slaw and fried potatoes on Italian bread — became the Steel City's signature culinary treat.

The unique delicacy has its roots in the mid-1930s, when a customer brought in some potatoes and wanted to know if they were frozen. The Primantis fried them. They looked good, and so they put them on a sandwich and liked the way it tasted.

Pittsburgh's hand-held gastronomic delight is a highlight of any visit to PNC Park, but it's just one of the local specialties.

The home of the Pirates offers an outstanding assortment of both traditional and regional ballpark foods. Those looking for classic baseball stadium fare will find everything they need at a food court called Pops' Plaza, which is named after seven-time All-Star Willie "Pops" Stargell, who led the Bucs to victory in the 1979 World Series.

Fans can also get a taste of Pittsburgh in another food court at the ballpark. This one, called Smorgasburgh, features local items like Quaker Steak and Benkovitz Fish, both from Western Pennsylvania restaurants. And, of course, a visitor can wash it all down with an Iron City Beer.

ROBERTO CLEMENTE BRIDGE

Throughout PNC Park there are tributes to Roberto Clemente, the Hall of Fame right fielder who died in a plane crash on Dec. 31, 1972, while on a mission to bring food and supplies to help people in earthquake-ravaged Nicaragua.

Aside from retiring Clemente's uniform number (21), PNC Park and the city of Pittsburgh also recognize the icon in another, less conventional, fashion.

On Aug. 6, 1998, the Sixth Street Bridge, one of three parallel bridges that cross the Allegheny River, was officially renamed the Roberto Clemente Bridge. The suspension bridge has a 442-foot main span, and is 884 feet in length, including the elevated ramps at each end. The crossing, which was built between 1925 and 1928, is 40 feet high.

Once across the bridge, fans are only a few steps from a Clemente statue, where he stands in the follow-through of a swing, hanging on to the bat in one hand as his body uncoils, ready to run to first base. Just months after his tragic death, the Baseball Writers Association of America waived the five-year waiting period and voted Clemente into the Hall of Fame in 1973.

Opening Day: July 23, 1923
Dimensions: LF: 312 ft.; CF: 430 ft.; RF: 347 ft.
First Pitch: Alex Kellner (KC)
First Home Run: Red Wilson (DET)
Also Known As: Muehlebach Field, Ruppert Stadium, Blues Stadium
Original Capacity: 17,500
Largest Capacity: 35,561
Cost: $400,000

MUNICIPAL STADIUM

From Muehlebach Field to Municipal Stadium, the name of the baseball park in Kansas City, Mo., changed almost as often as the clubs that played there. The structure existed for more than five decades and also served as the home field of four different professional baseball teams — the Kansas City Blues, a member of the American Association and a New York Yankees Minor League affiliate; the Kansas City Monarchs; the Athletics and the Kansas City Royals.

Originally named after Kansas City Blues Owner George Muehlebach — the hotel and beer magnate who built the stadium for the Blues — the ballpark grew from a single-tiered facility that had the capacity to seat 17,500 fans when it opened on July 23, 1923, to a 35,561-seat edifice when it hosted its last Big League game on Oct. 4, 1972. Before being purchased by the Yankees organization in 1938, the stadium was the site of the first Negro Leagues World Series.

By the time Opening Day 1955 had arrived, the park had become the home field for the Athletics franchise. Owner Arnold Johnson moved the team from Philadelphia to Kansas City after the '54 season. Johnson was responsible for increasing the capacity at the ballpark by adding an upper deck. Blues Stadium was also renamed Municipal Stadium at the beginning of that 1955 season.

1949 Kansas City Monarchs

MONARCHS DYNASTY

The Monarchs were one of the most successful teams in the Negro Leagues. The team operated from 1920 to 1960, winning 11 pennants during that stretch, the most of any Negro Leagues club.

The Monarchs boasted some of the greatest Negro Leagues players ever, including James "Cool Papa" Bell, Wilber Rogan, Jose Mendez, Hilton Smith and Buck O'Neil. But African-Americans were prevented from playing in the Major Leagues. It wasn't until

one-time Monarch Jackie Robinson broke the color barrier in 1947 that Negro Leaguers had the opportunity to reach the Big Leagues. Other Monarchs who eventually played in the Major Leagues included 1963 AL MVP Elston Howard, as well as Hall of Famers Ernie Banks and Willard Brown.

One of the most legendary Monarchs, and also one of the best pitchers in the history of the Negro Leagues, was Leroy

CHARLEY FINLEY AND THE PETTING ZOO

Major League Baseball officials didn't know what they were getting themselves into when they signed off on Charles Finley's purchase of the Kansas City Athletics in 1960. An eccentric showman and a savvy businessman, Finley was hardly the typical conservative team owner.

His contrarian's way carried over to the team's ballpark, where he made many changes during his tenure. Finley built a roof over the right-field corner, modeling it after Yankee Stadium's short right field. "Pennant Porch" hung over the field, shortening the home run distance, but league officials forced him to take it down. In defiance, Finley built a 40-foot screen on top of the right-field fence.

He also came up with the idea of "Harvey," a mechanical rabbit that popped up from under the ground around home plate at the touch of the umpire's foot to give him baseballs. Then there was Charley O, a mule that served as the team's mascot. Charley O and other four-legged animals, including sheep, grazed beyond the outfield in a tiny pasture that became a petting zoo for young fans.

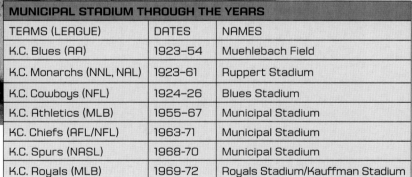

MUNICIPAL STADIUM THROUGH THE YEARS		
TEAMS (LEAGUE)	DATES	NAMES
K.C. Blues (AA)	1923–54	Muehlebach Field
K.C. Monarchs (NNL, NAL)	1923–61	Ruppert Stadium
K.C. Cowboys (NFL)	1924–26	Blues Stadium
K.C. Athletics (MLB)	1955–67	Municipal Stadium
KC Chiefs (AFL/NFL)	1963–71	Municipal Stadium
K.C. Spurs (NASL)	1968–70	Municipal Stadium
K.C. Royals (MLB)	1969–72	Royals Stadium/Kauffman Stadium

"Satchel" Paige. Throwing 64 consecutive scoreless innings at one stretch, Paige compiled an outstanding 31-4 record for the Pittsburgh Crawfords in 1933.

Paige finally made it to the Majors in 1948 when he was 42 years old. He went 28-31 with a 3.29 ERA for Cleveland, St. Louis and Kansas City, throwing his last Big League pitch in 1965 at the age of 59.

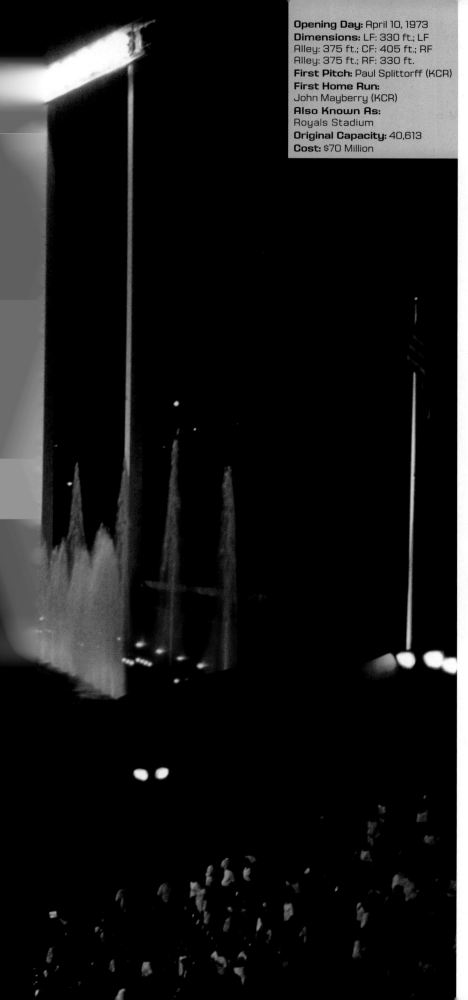

Opening Day: April 10, 1973
Dimensions: LF: 330 ft.; LF Alley: 375 ft.; CF: 405 ft.; RF Alley: 375 ft.; RF: 330 ft.
First Pitch: Paul Splittorff (KCR)
First Home Run: John Mayberry (KCR)
Also Known As: Royals Stadium
Original Capacity: 40,613
Cost: $70 Million

KAUFFMAN STADIUM

The expansion Kansas City Royals moved into Municipal Stadium in 1969, but they would only be temporary tenants — a home field of their own, Royals Stadium, was in the process of being built in another part of the city.

Located across the parking lot from Arrowhead Stadium, the home of the NFL's Kansas City Chiefs, Royals Owner Ewing Kauffman's ballpark opened on April 10, 1973. The stadium's baseball-specific nature was exciting for the Royals, as many other new stadiums of the time period, such as Shea Stadium of the New York Mets, had been built for the use of several different sports teams.

The ballpark was renamed Kauffman Stadium in July 1993, in honor of the team's owner who would die just one month later. It was also the first stadium in the American League to install Astroturf as its playing surface — a change that played a major role in the team's development, as it prompted scouts to watch for faster ballplayers, such as Willie Wilson, Amos Otis and Frank White. The artificial surface was replaced by natural grass in 1995.

Kauffman Stadium, the site of the 1973 All-Star Game, is widely considered to be one of the most architecturally beautiful sports venues in the country. The Royals' home provides fans the sight of a 322-foot water spectacular — the largest privately owned water fountain in the world.

.400 By George!

Brett

GEORGE BRETT AT THE PLATE IN 1980	
AVG	.390
RBI	118
H	175
HR	24
BB	58
OBP	.454
SLG	.664

CHASING .400

The incomparable Ted Williams batted .406 for the Red Sox in 1941. For the next 39 years, no player in the Major Leagues ended a season batting .400. But the Royals' George Brett got hot in 1980 — hotter than a scorching summer day in Kansas City — and made a strong charge at a magical .400 season.

The Royals third baseman was batting .337 at the All-Star break when he really caught fire. He got a hit in all but one of 21 games in July to post a torrid .494 average for the midsummer month. And Brett was almost as good in August, spraying hits to the tune of a .430 average. On Aug. 17, in front of 30,693 fans in Kansas City, he went 4 for 4 with two doubles and five RBI.

And Brett was doing all of this prodigious offensive damage despite suffering from torn ligaments in his right ankle. By Sept. 19, Brett had climbed back to the .400 mark. Sort of. His average was .3995, which rounded up to .400.

Unfortunately, he couldn't quite keep up the .400 pace, going 14 for 46 (.304) over his final 13 games, and ended the year at a highly respectable .390. He piled up 24 homers and 118 RBI to go with his impressive batting average, earning MVP honors in the American League and leading the Royals into the World Series, where they fell to the Phillies in six games. It was a memorable charge, but Williams' mark remained safe.

NOLAN RYAN'S FIRST GEM

Nolan Ryan's fastball blew by hitters like an express train, from his first days in the Big Leagues. As a rookie with the New York Mets in 1968, Ryan struck out 133 batters in 134 innings. He had trouble locating his pitches at times, though, as evidenced by the 75 walks he issued that year.

Wildness aside, there was no question that the flame-throwing right-hander was always tough to hit. And on May 15, 1973, in his sixth full Big League season and his second with the Angels, Ryan registered the first of seven career no-hitters, blanking the Kansas City Royals, 3-0.

The setting was Royals Stadium. The crowd was small; just 12,205 fans were on hand to witness Ryan's feat. Not that there had been any reason to expect greatness on this particular night. In his previous start, Ryan was tagged for five runs on four hits by the Chicago White Sox, and had been knocked out of the game after retiring just one hitter.

But against the Royals on this night, Ryan struck out three batters in the first inning. And the strikeouts just kept on coming. For a change, the number of walks he issued didn't keep pace. Ryan fanned 12 batters and walked just three, making it an easy night for his fielders. Shortstop Rudy Meoli fielded just one ball. And left fielder Vada Pinson didn't touch the ball at all defensively.

Ryan finished things off in the ninth inning. He retired Freddie Patek on a foul pop-up and then whiffed Steve Hovley. And when Amos Otis flied out, Ryan's first no-hitter was in the record books.

Ironically, Angels infielder Sandy Alomar Sr. made the first out of that game. And the batter who years later made the final out in Ryan's seventh and final no-hitter was Sandy's son, Roberto Alomar.

Orta (left)

CONTROVERSY AT FIRST

When people talk about the 1985 World Series, they don't begin by discussing John Tudor's Game 4 shutout for the Cardinals or Bret Saberhagen's five-hit shutout in the winner-take-all Game 7. Instead, the conversation almost always starts with a controversial umpire's call in the bottom of the ninth inning of Game 6 in Kansas City.

It appeared obvious that Jorge Orta was out when first baseman Jack Clark fielded a bouncing grounder and tossed to pitcher Todd Worrell at the bag. But it didn't look that way to first base umpire Don Denkinger, who incorrectly called Orta safe. The call gave the Royals, down 1-0 with three outs to play, new life.

And it clearly rattled St. Louis. Clark was unable to track down a subsequent foul ball, leading to a second-chance single by Steve Balboni. A one-out passed ball, an intentional walk and a looping two-run bases-loaded single by Dane Iorg gave the Royals an exhilarating 2-1 victory at suddenly raucous Royals Stadium that knotted the Series at three games apiece.

The next night the Royals crushed the dispirited Cardinals, 11-0, and claimed their first World Series crown. In doing so, Kansas City became the first team in World Series history to lose the first two games of the Fall Classic at home and come back to win it all.

O'Neil was one of the driving forces behind the creation of the Negro Leagues Baseball Museum in Kansas City

BUCK O'NEIL

There were few greater ambassadors for the game of baseball than John "Buck" O'Neil. A first baseman in the Negro Leagues, O'Neil played mostly for the Kansas City Monarchs during his 17-year career and went on to scout for the Chicago Cubs and Kansas City Royals after he hung up his spikes.

In his later years, he was one of the driving forces behind the creation of the Negro Leagues Baseball Museum in Kansas City, which was founded in 1990. He worked tirelessly to preserve the memories of the Negro Leagues.

After his death on Oct. 6, 2006, at the age of 94, the Royals established the Buck O'Neil Legacy Seat. It was April 2, 2007,

Opening Day at Kauffman Stadium, when ESPN broadcaster and Hall of Famer Joe Morgan announced the Royals' plan to choose someone each game worthy of filling Buck's seat, Section 101, Row C, Seat 1 — the one he sat in for so many Royals games as a scout and as a fan. That seat is painted bright red to stand out from the blue seats around it.

The team encourages community leaders to write to the ballclub and tell them why the nominee is worthy of filling Buck's seat. The tradition continued when the local cable network FSN Kansas City joined the effort by featuring the winners during game telecasts.

SPORTSMAN'S PARK

For years, there was hardly a line between entertainment and athletics at Sportsman's Park in St. Louis. Chris Von der Ahe, who owned the St. Louis Browns from 1882 to 1898, surrounded the facility with an amusement park and ran a beer garden and a horse track on the field of play.

Those wild days are but a footnote in the long, storied history of the site on the northeast corner of Grand Boulevard and Dodier Street, where baseball had been played since 1866. After suffering at least five fires in its history, Sportsman's Park was finally rebuilt as a fireproof concrete-and-steel structure. The Browns of the American League started to play there on April 14, 1909, and the National League's Cardinals joined them in 1920.

The Browns and Cardinals shared the park until 1953, when the AL club moved to Baltimore. Capacity at the stadium swelled to 34,023 when a second deck was added to the grandstand in 1926. August Busch bought the star-studded Cardinals that year, renamed the ballpark Busch Stadium and made a few renovations, including one signature addition: On the top of the scoreboard in left field, Busch, a beer magnate, installed the trademark Budweiser eagle, which flapped its wings each time a Cardinal hit a home run. It celebrated Cardinals longballs until the team moved to Busch Stadium II in 1966.

Opening Day: April 14, 1909
Dimensions: LF: 350 ft.; LF
Alley: 414 ft.; CF: 445 ft.; RF: 315 ft.
First Pitch: Jack Powell (STL)
First Home Run:
Danny Hoffman (STL)
Also Known As:
Grand Avenue Ball Grounds
Original Capacity: 24,040
Largest Capacity: 34,023
Cost: $300,000

PAVILION

STAN 'THE MAN' MUSIAL

Stan Musial got his nickname, "The Man," from reverential opposing fans at the Brooklyn Dodgers' Ebbets Field. When he stepped up to the plate, the fans were known to yell, "Uh, oh, here comes the man again!" But it was on his home turf, Sportsman's Park in St. Louis, that Musial's amazing consistency as a hitter stamped him as one of the game's all-time greatest ballplayers.

The native of Donora, Pa., played the outfield as well as first base, but was far better known for his work in the batter's box, finishing with 3,630 career hits and a .331 overall average. Musial, who played his entire 22-year career with St. Louis, helped lead the Cardinals to world championships in 1942, '44 and '46. He was also a three-time National League MVP, a seven-time batting champ and was voted an All-Star 24 times. His career came to an end in 1963, and he was honored as a first-ballot Hall of Fame inductee in 1969.

Musial was the first member of the Cardinals franchise to have his uniform number retired, and a bronze statue of the superstar was erected at the entrance of Busch Stadium II in 1968. Its inscription reads: "Here stands baseball's perfect warrior. Here stands baseball's perfect knight."

Slaughter

SLAUGHTER'S MAD DASH

The 1946 World Series was knotted at three games apiece. And the decisive Game 7 was tied, 3-3, in the bottom of the eighth when Enos "Country" Slaughter laced a leadoff single to center off Boston's Bob Klinger. Slaughter lingered at first base as Klinger retired the next two hitters, but with Harry "The Hat" Walker at the plate, Slaughter took off for second on a stolen-base attempt. With Slaughter running, Walker smacked the pitch into left-center. Slaughter steamed around second base as Red Sox outfielder Leon Culberson picked up the ball, bobbled it momentarily and threw to his relay man, shortstop Johnny Pesky.

Cardinals third-base coach Mike Gonzalez signaled to hold up at third, but Slaughter ignored him, raced around the bag and headed home. Out in his cutoff position, Pesky, like most everyone else at Sportsman's Park, never expected Slaughter to try for home. By the time Pesky fired the ball, it was too late. Slaughter slid safely across the plate, his daring move providing the winning run for St. Louis.

After the game, Slaughter said that scoring on the play was a no-brainer. His dash around the bases electrified the 36,143 fans at Sportsman's Park and sparked St. Louis to a 4-3 win and its third world championship in five years.

"It was a gutsy play," Slaughter said. "But you know, two men out and the winning run, you can't let grass grow under your feet."

1944 World Series

ST. LOUIS SHOWDOWN

A Cardinals appearance in the World Series was not all that un-usual. The St. Louis Browns in the Series? That was peculiar. But in 1944, Sportsman's Park was the site of an all-St. Louis battle for the world championship crown, when the Browns and their tenants, the Cardinals, met up in the Fall Classic. The AL team was a serious underdog, with just one player hitting above .300 (with a .301 average) and one man who hit 20 home runs.

Major League Baseball had lost many of its best players en-tering the 1944 season because of World War II. As a result, the Browns managed to reach the World Series for the first — and only — time in their 52-year history. The Cardinals, meanwhile,

claimed their third straight NL pennant and eighth in the club's previous 19 years.

The Browns got off to a great start in what was called the "St. Louis Showdown." Between 31,360 and 36,568 fans packed into Sportsman's Park for each game of the Series, more of them Browns fans than Cardinals backers. The Browns thanked the fans for their support by winning Games 1 and 3 for a 2-games-to-1 lead in the Series.

Those early wins, though, would be the Series highlight for the Browns. The Cardinals won the final three games to earn their second World Series title in three years.

Gaedel

THE SMALLEST PINCH-HITTER

Bill Veeck was a showman, always trying to find ways to drum up publicity and boost attendance for his baseball teams. In 1951, Veeck owned the St. Louis Browns.

On Aug. 19, he signed Eddie Gaedel, who stood just 3-foot-7, to a Big League contract. Gaedel's first appearance came between games of a doubleheader against the Tigers. Veeck rolled a cake out to home plate and Gaedel jumped out, generating surprise and cheers from the crowd.

During the second game, Veeck sent Gaedel, wearing the number 1/8 on his back, to pinch-hit, having instructed him not to swing the bat. Gaedel went into his stance, crouching down low, and giving Detroit pitcher Bob Cain a roughly one-foot strike zone. Cain walked Gaedel on four pitches, each of which was — predictably— high.

American League officials were not amused. They voided Gaedel's contract, and re-moved the at-bat from the record books, though Gaedel's plate appearance was restored the following year, giving him a career on-base percentage of 1.000.

ST. LOUIS BROWNS CLUB TIMELINE

April 1902: Former Milwaukee Brewers debut at Sports-man's Park as the Browns

1916: Owner Robert Lee Hedges sells team to Philip DeCatesby Ball

1925: Ball expands capacity of Sportsman's to 30,500

1953: Club moves to Baltimore. Sportsman's is renamed Busch Stadium

1909: Browns rebuild a fireproof Sportsman's Park

1920: Browns share Sportsman's with Cardinals after they move from Robinson Field

1951: Bill Veeck purchases Browns

BUSCH STADIUM II

The Cardinals moved out of Busch Stadium, formerly known as Sportsman's Park, early in the 1966 season, and were playing games at their next home field just four days later. Busch Stadium II would be the club's home through four memorable decades. Although St. Louis later moved into a new park in 2006 — Busch Stadium III, which hosted a World Series win that year — Busch Stadium II served the club well. As multi-purpose parks of the "cookie-cutter" era went, Busch Stadium II was one of the nicest, with an open-scallop design along the roof, mirroring the city's Gateway Arch.

Due to the park's multi-purpose nature, the playing surface underwent occasional changes. The natural grass surface was switched to AstroTurf in 1970, allowing for an easier switch from baseball to football use.

In 1995, the NFL's Cardinals left St. Louis, and owners of the baseball team replaced the turf with natural grass. The new baseball-only park also saw the addition of new seating and scoreboards. Outside, in the Plaza of Champions, statues of Bob Gibson, Lou Brock, Enos Slaughter, Red Schoendienst and Jack Buck were erected.

St. Louis beat the Red Sox in the World Series in 1967, their first full year in Busch Stadium II. But they weren't as successful in the last Fall Classic there, getting swept by the Sox in 2004. The park was demolished in 2005.

Opening Day: May 12, 1966
Dimensions: LF: 330 ft.; LF Alley: 372 ft.; CF: 402 ft.; RF Alley: 372 ft.; RF: 330 ft.
First Pitch: Ray Washburn (STL)
First Home Run: Felipe Alou (ATL)
Also Known As: Civic Center, Busch Memorial Stadium
Original Capacity: 46,068
Largest Capacity: 50,435
Cost: $20 Million

Buck

VOICE OF ST. LOUIS

Jack Buck's voice became synonymous with Cardinals baseball during his storied 46-year broadcasting career. He annually worked national radio and television broadcasts of Super Bowl and World Series games. But Buck wasn't just an announcer. He was part of the game in St. Louis.

Known for his wit, Buck's ability to capture the moment clearly in a few sharp and descriptive words set him apart from his colleagues. His enthusiasm made his calls memorable. St. Louis fans won't soon forget the time Ozzie Smith lofted a key home run in the 1985 NLCS. "Go crazy, folks! Go crazy! It's a home run!" Buck roared.

In 1987, the Baseball Hall of Fame honored him with the Ford C. Frick Award. The Cardinals honored Buck, who passed away in 2002, with a bronze sculpture of his likeness behind a microphone.

SWALLOWED BY A TARP

Injuries are part of the game, but Cardinals outfielder Vince Coleman suffered an unusual and unnecessary one as he stood on the Busch Stadium field before Game 4 of the 1985 NLCS against the Los Angeles Dodgers.

The 101-win Cardinals had dropped Games 1 and 2 in Los Angeles, but taken the third contest back at Busch Stadium. Coleman, with 110 stolen bases and 170 hits during the regular season of his rookie year, including 10 triples and 20 doubles, was supposed to play a key role in helping St. Louis even up the Series.

It was drizzling as Coleman stood on the first-base side of the Astroturf field, and the stadium grounds crew began to roll up the electronically controlled tarp, which had been pro-

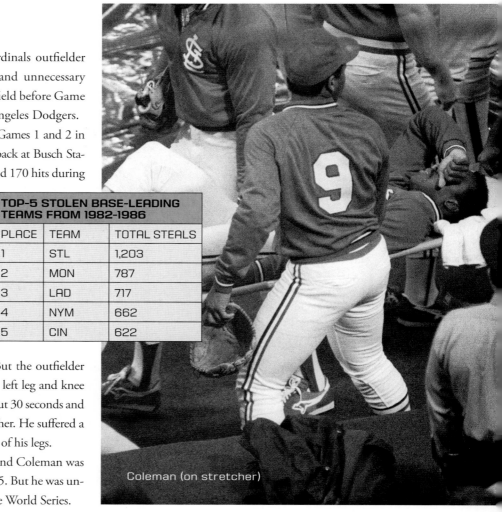

Coleman (on stretcher)

TOP-5 STOLEN BASE-LEADING TEAMS FROM 1982-1986

PLACE	TEAM	TOTAL STEALS
1	STL	1,203
2	MON	787
3	LAD	717
4	NYM	662
5	CIN	622

tecting the field during the warm-up. But the outfielder didn't see it moving toward him, and his left leg and knee became caught in it. He was stuck for about 30 seconds and had to be taken from the field on a stretcher. He suffered a bone chip in his knee and bruises on one of his legs.

St. Louis took the pennant anyway, and Coleman was still named the Rookie of the Year of 1985. But he was unable to return in the NLCS or play in the World Series.

Gibson

WORLD SERIES HERO

Bob Gibson was solid in the 1964 World Series for the Cardinals, but in 1967 and '68, after the St. Louis franchise had packed up and moved from Sportsman's Park to Busch Stadium, the right-hander was as dominant as any pitcher in the history of the Fall Classic.

In 1967, Gibson nearly single-handedly toppled the Red Sox for the championship. An intense competitor with a blazing fastball, Gibson allowed just three earned runs in fashioning three complete-game wins, including a triumph in the deciding Game 7. He surrendered just 14 hits and five walks, striking out 26 in his 27 innings.

The Cards' right-hander was just about as dominant the following year, but St. Louis came up short in the end against Detroit in seven games. In the 1968 Series, Gibson went 2-1 with a 1.67 ERA. He gave up 18 hits and walked just four, fanning an astounding 35 Tigers in 27 innings pitched, including a record 17 in Game 1. Gibson went head to head against Mickey Lolich in the deciding game, but Lolich defied the odds, giving Detroit its first championship since 1945.

Smith

OZZIE SMITH

SS

CARDINAL

UNLIKELY POWER SURGE

When Ozzie Smith came to bat in a tied Game 5, 3-3, with one out in the bottom of the ninth of the 1985 NLCS at Busch Stadium, the Dodgers were worried about him reaching first and stealing a base or two. Rightfully so, as the 30-year-old went on to put up a .500 on-base percentage for the Series and a .435 average, ultimately going 10 for 23 with three walks. The Dodgers were not, however, worried about him homering to win the game.

To everyone's surprise at Busch Stadium, Smith lofted a drive to right field that caromed off the facing of the lower deck. The bomb gave St. Louis a 4-3 victory over a stunned Tom Niedenfuer and the Dodgers, and sparked the Cards to the NL pennant.

It would be Smith's only home run in his 144 postseason at-bats, which came in eight series over 19 years.

In 2005, that home run by Smith was voted by fans as the greatest moment in the history of Busch Stadium.

THE CHASE

When the Cardinals acquired Mark McGwire from Oakland on July 31, 1997, they figured they were guaranteed to add power to the lineup. They had no idea that they were obtaining a man who would not only chase Roger Maris's record for home runs in a single season, but who would also shatter the record, becoming a folk hero in St. Louis along the way.

McGwire slugged 24 homers for the Cardinals in the last two months of 1997, and then, after signing with the team as a free agent, turned Busch Stadium into his own personal Little League field, clearing the fences with ease and frequency during a record-setting 1998 campaign.

McGWIRE'S SPIKES

By Aug. 19, McGwire had slugged 49 homers, one more than the Cubs' Sammy Sosa, in a race to pass Maris's record of 61, which had been set in 1961.

On Sept. 8, 1998, McGwire blasted a pitch from the Cubs' Steve Trachsel over the left-field wall at Busch Stadium for his record-breaking 62nd homer of the season. He put the finishing touches on his feat with a wild celebration at home plate that included a hug for his son, who was serving as a batboy.

McGwire would go on to extend his record to 70 regular-season home runs. That mark was eclipsed by San Francisco's big slugger Barry Bonds, who blasted 73 longballs in his record-breaking 2001 season. McGwire was beloved in St. Louis. He launched 65 homers in 1999, 32 in 2000 and 29 in 2001, with injuries hampering him over his final two seasons and forcing him into retirement after the 2001 campaign.

McGwire finished his career with 583 homers, including the 220 he hit for the Cardinals in just four-plus seasons.

McGwire

Opening Day: April 12, 1909
Dimensions: LF: 378 ft.;
CF: 515 ft.; RF: 340 ft.
First Pitch:
Eddie Plank (PHA)
First Home Run:
Frank Baker (PHA)
Also Known As:
Connie Mack Stadium
Original Capacity: 20,000
Largest Capacity: 33,000
Cost: $457,168

CHAPTER 4

OLDIES
BUT GOODIES

SHIBE PARK

When Shibe Park opened in North Philadelphia on April 12, 1909, it was a departure from the wooden stadiums that housed all other Big League teams. The fireproof concrete-and-steel design would be emulated consistently during the following decades.

Fans marveled at Shibe Park's French Renaissance-style brick-and-stone facade. The ballpark was an architectural masterpiece, complete with dormer windows, arches, flat columns, a circular corner entrance and a cupola dome that housed the office of Manager Connie Mack, who helped design the edifice with owner Ben Shibe.

The Athletics built the new ball-park to take advantage of recent success, having captured the AL pennant in 1902 and 1905, led by hurlers Rube Waddell and Eddie Plank. Shibe boasted a double-deck grandstand behind home plate, stretching from foul pole to foul pole. It could accommodate 23,000 fans, in comparison to 13,600 at the team's former home, Columbia Park. Shibe was the first ballpark to seat as many as 20,000 fans.

In 1935, the right-field fence was raised from 12 to 34 feet to keep people from sitting on nearby rooftops and viewing games free of charge. It was called a "spite fence" by the fans.

Philadelphia A's celebrate
during 1929 World Series.
Inset: Fans pack roofs
outside Shibe Park during
1929 World Series.

1929 WORLD SERIES

The Chicago Cubs held an 8-0 lead over the A's heading into the bottom of the seventh inning of Game 4 of the 1929 World Series at Shibe Park. The visitors were on the verge of knotting the Fall Classic at two games apiece.

The Athletics, though, were not ready to surrender Game 4, or their lead in the Series. Al Simmons led off the bottom of the seventh inning by blasting a homer off Charlie Root, a titanic shot that landed on the left-field roof. Jimmie Foxx came up next and singled, and Bing Miller followed suit, his fly ball dropping in when Hack Wilson lost it in the sun. Both Jimmy Dykes and Joe Boley reached on base hits, cutting the Cubs' lead to 8-3. Next, Max Bishop's one-out RBI single knocked Root from the game. His replacement, Art Nehf, didn't fare much better. Mule Haas smacked a three-run inside-the-park homer, and suddenly the Cubs' lead was just one run. After a walk, Nehf was lifted for John Blake. Simmons and Foxx, batting for the second time in the inning, each greeted Blake with singles, tying the game, 8-8. The Cubs brought in pitcher Pat Malone to stem the tide, but he hit a batter and was tagged for a two-run double by Dykes that capped the A's explosion.

The Athletics' 10 runs in the seventh inning amounted to the biggest comeback in World Series history. The A's 10-8 victory shocked the Cubs and gave Philadelphia a commanding 3-games-to-1 lead in the World Series. Connie Mack's Athletics would win the next contest to capture the world championship.

Mack

CONNIE MACK

The Athletics of the fledgling American League offered Cornelius "Connie" Mack a deal he couldn't pass up. A journeyman catcher and eventual player-manager during his career, Mack had just three seasons of full-time managerial experience when the A's offered him that role for their club — along with a 25 percent ownership stake in the franchise. Mack would become a fixture in the home dugout at Shibe Park for the next half-century. Always nattily attired in suit jacket and tie with a straw hat, Mack was known for his gentlemanly demeanor, but also his ability to maintain discipline.

As part owner of the Athletics, Mack's responsibility of the team's financial viability led him to trade away some of his better players over the years in an effort to keep the team solvent. His frugality accounts for the many last-place finishes suffered by the Athletics — which were balanced out by some stretches when the team was the most dominant in the Majors. From 1910 to 1913, the Athletics won three world championships. And they won three consecutive American League pennants from 1929 to 1931, taking the World Series in 1929 and 1930.

Mack, regarded as one of the game's greatest tacticians, captured nine pennants and five World Series crowns during his tenure with Philadelphia. He was considered such a great manager that he was inducted into the Hall of Fame in 1937, 13 years before he retired after the 1950 season.

OLDIES BUT GOODIES

COMISKEY PARK

The innovative symmetry of Comiskey Park's playing surface, highly unusual for the time, was achieved by architect Zachary Taylor Davis. And the field's large proportions were the work of Chicago White Sox hurler Ed Walsh, who was asked by Owner Charles Comiskey to help design the new facility. Walsh, having already won 110 games for the White Sox before the start of the 1910 season when Comiskey Park debuted, was instrumental in turning the South Side stadium into a pitcher's park. The spacious dimensions in the stadium's outfield surrendered just three home runs in 1910.

The original Comiskey Park was a 28,800-seat facility built on a former city landfill site. Made with fireproof steel and concrete, it was built just about one year after Shibe Park and Forbes Field, the first ballparks to feature the predominantly woodless design. Its grand opening in July 1910, ironically, was ultimately compromised by a steelworkers' strike.

In contrast to its understated red brick facade, the ballpark was home to the one-of-a-kind showman Bill Veeck, who owned the team twice, from 1959 to 1961 and again from 1975 to 1981.

Among the many promotional stunts that he tried at Comiskey, Veeck installed an exploding scoreboard in center field, complete with spinning pinwheels and fireworks that went off whenever the White Sox hit a home run.

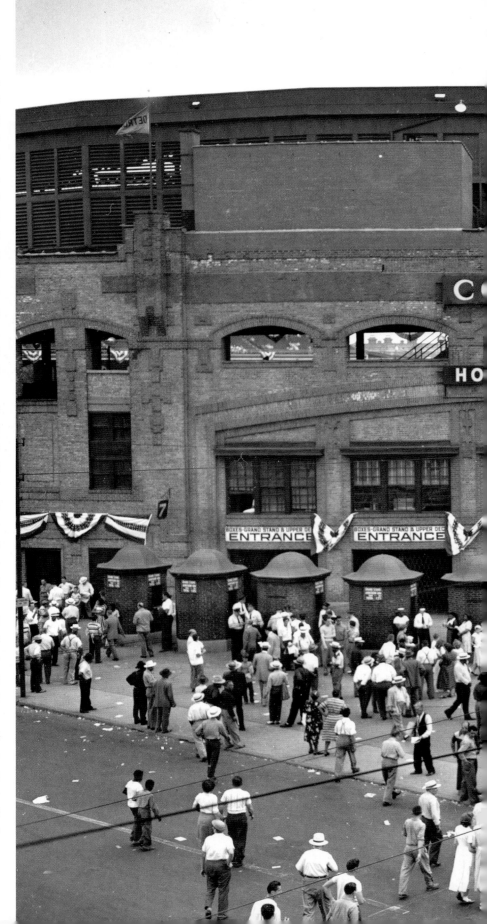

Opening Day: July 1, 1910
Dimensions: LF: 363 ft.;
LF Alley: 382 ft.; CF: 420 ft.;
RF Alley: 382 ft.; RF: 363 ft.
First Pitch: Ed Walsh (CHW)
First Home Run: Lee
Tannehill (CHW)
Original Capacity: 28,800
Largest Capacity: 52,000
Cost: $750,000

Caray (left), White Sox
Manager Chuck Tanner

THE VOICE OF CHICAGO

Chicago White Sox broadcaster Harry Caray had a habit of singing along with long-time Comiskey Park organist Nancy Faust's rendition of "Take Me Out to the Ballgame" during the seventh-inning stretch. Few people knew about this until, unbeknownst to Caray, the broadcast booth's microphones were open during one of his performances and all of Comiskey Park was allowed to listen. While Caray's singing may not have earned him a gig at the Chicago Theater, it did manage to spawn a Big League tradition: What began as one man's idiosyncratic serenade at Comiskey Park became a staple at every ballpark.

Caray, who began his Major League broadcasting career with his hometown St. Louis Cardinals in 1945, spent one season with the Oakland A's before joining the Sox in 1971. The ebullient voice of the Midwest spent 11 seasons at Comiskey Park before a dispute led him to take his seventh-inning tradition with him to Wrigley Field on the north side of Chicago after the 1981 season.

Never missing a game during his first 41 seasons in the booth, Caray's devotion to the home team made him a fan favorite throughout his 52-year career in the Big Leagues. Named Baseball Broadcaster of the Year seven consecutive times by *The Sporting News*, Caray received the Ford C. Frick Award from the Baseball Hall of Fame in 1989.

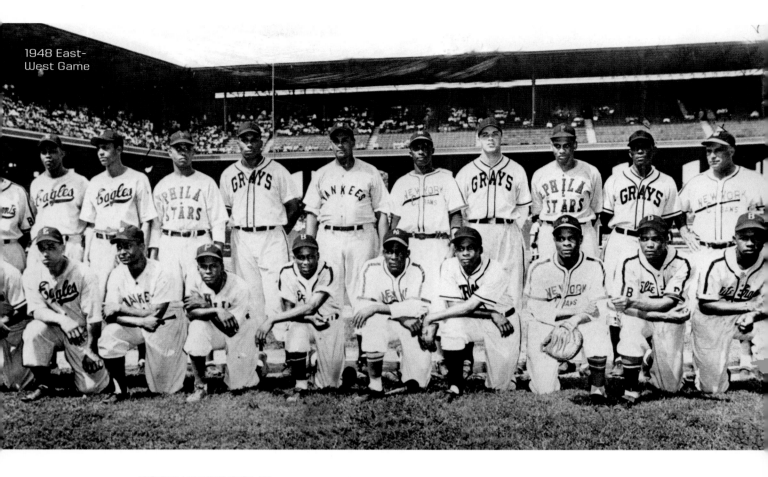

EAST-WEST GAME

When Roy Sparrow, the traveling secretary for the Pittsburgh Crawfords of the Negro National League, first heard about the Major League All-Star Game scheduled for July 1933, he decided the Negro Leagues should explore the concept as well. On Sept. 10, 1933, just two months after Babe Ruth headlined the all-white All-Star Game at Comiskey Park, Sparrow watched as the best players in the Negro Leagues took the same field for the first East-West Game. While the Major Leagues' Midsummer Classic was sponsored by the *Chicago Tribune*, this exhibition was sponsored by the *Chicago Defender* and the *Pittsburgh Courier*, a pair of African-American weeklies.

The East-West Game couldn't have debuted under more difficult circumstances, as America was in the midst of the Great Depression. Yet, in the midst of some ill-timed rain, more than 20,000 fans attended that inaugural contest, which featured Josh Gibson, Bill Foster and Oscar Charleston.

Many African-American families soon planned vacations around the annual game. It even boasted higher attendance than the Major Leagues' All-Star Game nine times within an 18-year period. The East-West Game featured notable players over the years, including Jackie Robinson, who represented the Kansas City Monarchs in 1945. The final East-West Game was played in 1958, with each contest having been played at Comiskey Park.

GRIFFITH STADIUM

On St. Patrick's Day 1911, the Washington Senators were away at Spring Training. National Park, located on the corner of Georgia Avenue and W Street NW in the nation's capital, meanwhile, was burning to the ground.

With the season set to begin in a matter of weeks, construction began immediately on a new park for the Senators. Although efficiency was of paramount importance, the park was built with concrete and steel, following the lead of several recently constructed fireproof stadiums.

Just five months later, the Senators opened their new park, which featured double-decked stands extending around home plate from first base to third base. The spacious new National Park was renamed Griffith Stadium in 1922 when former Big League pitcher and manager Clark Griffith bought the team.

Despite the initial rush to build the venue, the Senators' new home field managed to have a number of unique features. Most important was the addition of the presidential box, which was located along the first-base line. William Howard Taft began the tradition of the president of the United States throwing out the first pitch on Opening Day when he did so at Griffith Stadium on April 14, 1910. Nine U.S. presidents would throw out a pitch at Griffith Stadium before it closed for good in 1961.

Opening Day: April 12, 1911
Dimensions: LF: 407 ft.; LF Alley: 393 ft.; CF: 421 ft.; RF Alley: 405 ft.; RF: 280 ft.
First Pitch: Dolly Gray (WAS)
First Home Run: Eddie Collins (PHA)
Also Known As: National Park
Original Capacity: 32,000

Mantle (right)

TAPE-MEASURE BLAST

With a runner on first and two outs in the top of the fifth inning on April 17, 1953, Mickey Mantle stepped into the batter's box against Washington Senators pitcher Chuck Stobbs. It was the two-year anniversary of Mantle's Big League debut, and he crushed Stobbs' 1-and-0 offering. The ball sailed over the fence in left-center (about 391 feet from the plate), over the bleachers (460 feet from the plate), over a wall (55 feet high), nicked the National Bohemian beer sign above the wall, and landed in the backyard of a house at 434 Oakdale St., across from the stadium.

Red Patterson, the Yankees' PR director, coined the expression "tape-measure homer" trying to chronicle the length of the blast. The accuracy of Patterson's 565-foot designation is debatable since it was unclear whether he used an actual tape measure or if he walked off the distance from the wall to the spot where the ball landed, but fans at the game could verify that Mantle's blast did, indeed, fly out of Griffith Stadium.

Johnson

THE BIG TRAIN ARRIVES

During the Washington franchise's early years, the teams that played at National Park were hardly dominant, leading the *San Francisco Chronicle* to declare Washington, "first in war, first in peace and last in the American League."

Walter Johnson was often the sole bright spot during those seasons gone off the tracks. The long-limbed hurler, dubbed "The Big Train," won 33 games in 1912, 36 in 1913 and at least 20 in 10 other years. Finally, in 1924 — Johnson's 18th season — the Senators reached the World Series for the first time, thanks in part to Johnson's 23 wins that season.

After waiting so long for a chance in the Fall Classic, Johnson's first two World Series outings weren't pleasant experiences. The Senators lost Game 1, 4-3, in 12 innings to the New York Giants, with Johnson going the distance. The Big Train was then derailed in a Game 5 loss, battered for 13 hits in a 6-2 setback.

The Series, though, went seven games. After Washington tied the deciding game in the eighth, Senators player-manager Bucky Harris brought in Johnson, who worked out of numerous jams to author four scoreless frames.

Then in the 12th, Giants catcher Hank Gowdy tripped over his mask in a failed attempt to catch Muddy Ruel's foul pop-up, and Ruel then ripped a double. Shortstop Travis Jackson bobbled a grounder hit by Johnson; Earl McNeely then bounced a single over third baseman Freddy Lindstrom. The Senators scored a 4-3 win.

And like that, Johnson was the winning pitcher in the decisive game as the Senators claimed their only world championship.

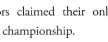

Opening Day: May 16, 1871
Dimensions: LF: 250 ft.;
LF Alley: 445 ft.; CF: 500 ft.;
RF Alley: 440 ft.; RF: 255 ft.
Original Capacity: 6,800
Largest Capacity: 11,000

SOUTH END GROUNDS

The Fenway district of Boston stretches north from Mission Hill to Columbus Avenue. From 1871 to 1914, there were three ballparks on a patch of land at the northeast corner of Columbus Avenue and Walpole Street, an area referred to as the South End Grounds. Boston's home for National League baseball, the South End Grounds was across the New York, New Haven and Hartford Railroad tracks from the Huntington Avenue Grounds, home of the AL's Red Sox.

The original South End Grounds opened on May 16, 1871, and was demolished on Sept. 10, 1887. The next incarnation of the South End Grounds was so magnificent that it was called the "Grand Pavilion." A baseball palace, the architecture included medieval-style turrets on the grandstand roof.

Unfortunately, the lavish ballpark was destroyed in the Great Roxbury Fire in 1894. Reportedly started by youngsters underneath the right-field bleachers, the blaze claimed 177 buildings.

South End Grounds III opened on July 20, 1894, and also looked like a castle, but it was far more Spartan upon entering. Insufficient insurance on South End Grounds II had left the club incapable of reproducing the "Grand Pavilion."

Boston's Senior Circuit squad went by several informal names, including the Beaneaters, before settling on the Braves. The club played its last game at the ballpark on Aug. 11, 1914.

THE 'MIRACLE' BRAVES

On July 4 it looked to fans at the South End Grounds as if 1914 would be another lost year for the Boston Braves, who were in last place, 14 games under .500 and 15 games behind the Giants.

Given the circumstances, no one thought much of the team's 1-0 win over Cincinnati on July 17. But Boston went on to win the next day. And the next day, too. Out of nowhere, the Braves won six in a row, climbing into fourth place.

The climb continued throughout the second half of the year, with the season's pivotal point occurring on Labor Day weekend. Boston hosted the New York Giants for a series at Fenway — the Braves moved from the South End Grounds to the Red Sox's park after Aug. 11, since it could hold larger crowds. The Braves and Giants split a Labor Day doubleheader, but Boston won the series finale the next day and moved ahead of New York for good.

1914
Braves

The "Miracle" Braves went 68-19 after July 4 — then the largest comeback in Big League history — and swept Connie Mack's Philadelphia A's for the world championship.

1914 BOSTON BRAVES SEASON RESULTS						
W	L	PCT	GB	ATTENDANCE	HITS	RUNS SCORED
94	59	.614	-	382,913	1,307	657

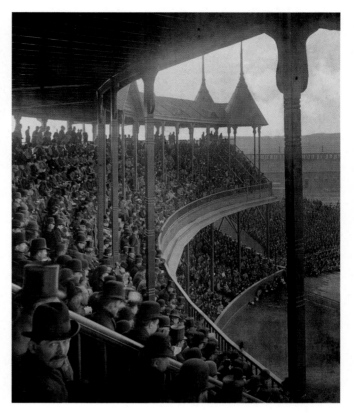

AN OPENING DAY TO REMEMBER

There was a sense of optimism in the South End Grounds on April 19, 1900. It was Opening Day, and the Boston Beaneaters figured to challenge for the NL pennant. Although they had fallen short of the Brooklyn Dodgers in 1899, Boston had raised the championship banner in the two years prior to that. All the seats were filled, and standing-room tickets had to be sold, permitting fans to watch the game from a roped-off area in deep center field. A special ground rule had to be enacted for the day — any ball bouncing past the rope would be a single.

To the dismay of the crowd, the visiting Phillies jumped out to an early lead and eventually expanded it to 16-4. Heading into the bottom of the ninth, Philadelphia still seemed comfortably ahead, 17-8.

But the Beaneaters didn't give in. Boston pinch-hitter Buck Freeman opened the bottom of the ninth inning with a home run, and by the time Philadelphia's starting pitcher Al Orth got the final out of the frame, nine baserunners had crossed the plate, tying the game, 17-17. Alas, the late rally didn't spur Boston to victory. The Phillies tallied a pair of runs in the 10th and held Boston off for a memorable 19-17 Opening Day win at the South End Grounds.

BRAVES FIELD

Although the fences at Braves Field seemed to change regularly, it was still a rare feat to hit a home run that cleared the outfield wall during the first few decades of Big League play at the home of the Boston Braves. When the park opened in 1915 the fences measured 402 feet down the left-field line and a whopping 461 to straightaway center field.

And the dimensions weren't all that was oversized about the ballpark. When it opened on Aug. 18, 1915, Braves Field was the first stadium to seat 40,000. The park accommodated 18,000 fans from foul line to foul line, 20,000 more in various areas behind the fences in right and left fields, and another 2,000 in center-field stands called the "Jury Box," so nicknamed after a sportswriter counted just 12 fans seated in the section during a sparsely attended midweek game.

The AL's Red Sox even played the 1915 and 1916 Fall Classics at Braves Field because they could draw larger crowds than at the smaller Fenway Park.

After the 1927 season, 6,000 seats were added in left and center fields as the fences were brought in to 353 feet in left and 387 in center.

Braves Field was sold to Boston University before the start of the 1953 season, after the franchise moved to Milwaukee. Boston University's Nickerson Field took the stadium's place on the site.

Opening Day: August 18, 1915
Dimensions: LF: 402.5 ft.; LF Alley: 402.5 ft.; CF: 461 ft.; RF Alley: 542 ft.; RF: 375 ft.
First Pitch: Dick Rudolph (BOS)
First Home Run: Doc Johnston (PIT)
Also Known As: National League Park, Nickerson Field
Original Capacity: 40,000
Largest Capacity: 46,000

Feller

GAME 1 THRILLER

Game 1 of the 1948 World Series between the Cleveland Indians and Boston Braves was a taut, scoreless affair when Indians ace Bob Feller went back out to the mound in the bottom of the eighth at Braves Field.

Feller, who had allowed just one hit up to that point, walked Bill Salkeld, the leadoff batter in that inning. Phil Masi went in to run for Salkeld and was sacrificed over to second by outfielder Mike McCormick. With first base open, Feller and the Indians elected to give Eddie Stanky an intentional pass, setting up a potential double play opportunity.

With Tommy Holmes up, Feller suddenly whirled around and quickly threw to player-manager Lou Boudreau at second base in an attempt to pick off Masi. It was a close play. Many at the ballpark thought Masi was out, but umpire Bill Stewart was not one of them. He called Masi safe.

Despite Boudreau's ardent protests, Stewart didn't change his call. Feller then pitched to Holmes, who banged a single. Masi came around to score.

The run held up as the only one of the game as the Braves, behind the performance of right-hander Johnny Sain, beat the Indians, 1-0, in the Series opener. Buoyed by the Game 1 win, the Braves went on to a six-game victory over Cleveland for the World Series crown.

SPAHN AND SAIN

Gerald V. Hern, sports editor of the *Boston Post*, penned a poem in 1948 to honor the ace hurlers who led the Braves pitching staff. The 31-word poem was often reduced to the catchy phrase, "Spahn and Sain and pray for rain."

Hern was writing about left-hander Warren Spahn and right-hander Johnny Sain, the pair who carried the Braves down the stretch of the '48 pennant race.

The Braves swept a doubleheader on Labor Day. In the first game, Spahn pitched a 14-inning complete game for a win, and Sain followed with a shutout victory in the nightcap. After two days off and two rainouts, the pair again swept a doubleheader, with Sain winning, 3-1, and Spahn, 13-2. Three days later, Spahn again was a winner, and once again Sain won the next day. After one day off, Spahn and Sain each won a game in a doubleheader, making them a combined 8-0 in a 13-day span and sparking a surge to the club's first pennant since the Miracle Braves in 1914.

"Spahn & Sain"
by Gerald Hern

First we'll use Spah[n]
then we'll use Sain
Then an off day
followed by rain
Back will come Spa[hn]
followed by Sain
And followed
we hope
by two days of rain

Spahn (left),
Sain

CROSLEY FIELD

As the Cincinnati Reds' fan base grew, the team was forced to abandon the Palace of the Fans, its lavish ballpark that featured luxury boxes and Greek columns. The team moved into the larger Redland Field on April 12, 1912. Even if the new park, which was renamed Crosley Field in 1934, wasn't as ornately designed as its predecessor, it still had numerous memorable elements of its own.

One of Crosley Field's unique aspects was the "Sun Deck," a trapeziod-shaped portion of the bleachers in right field that intersected the center-field fence. A line was painted on the concrete at that spot. Ground rules stated that any fly ball that hit the wall to the right of the line was a home run.

There was also the small sign above the roof in left-center field that read: "Hit this sign and get a Siebler suit free." Wally Post was the unofficial team leader in free suits won, with 16.

While lights had been used to play night baseball at Minor League parks for about five years, it wasn't until May 24, 1935, that the Majors' first night game was played at Crosley Field.

Crosley's last game was June 24, 1970, and it was a memorable one. The Reds were trailing, 4-3, to Hall of Fame right-hander Juan Marichal and the Giants, but won the game, 5-4, on back-to-back eighth-inning homers by Hall of Fame catcher Johnny Bench and first baseman Lee May.

Opening Day: April 12, 1912
Dimensions: LF: 360 ft.; LF Alley: 380 ft.; CF: 420 ft.; RF Alley: 383 ft.; RF: 400 ft.
First Pitch: Frank Smith (CIN)
First Home Run: Jimmy Esmond (CIN)
Also Known As: Redland Field
Original Capacity: 25,000
Largest Capacity: 33,000
Cost: $225,000

'THE TERRACE'

There were several challenges when it came to playing left field at Crosley Field. First, there was the flagpole in play out in left-center field, and then there was the portion of the outfield called "The Terrace."

Ballparks built during the early years of the 20th century did not have dirt warning tracks at the edges of the outfield grass to alert fielders that they were approaching the fence, which in those days tended to be hard brick without any padding. In an

effort to provide some warning, many fields had outfields that sloped up to meet the fence. The slope of the incline approaching the wall at Crosley Field was 15 degrees. Beginning about 20 feet away from the outfield wall, the field gradually rose until it reached a four-foot grade at the base of the wall.

Outfielders at Crosley Field would sometimes lose their footing trying to keep their eyes on the ball as they ran uphill. Babe Ruth was one such player. On May 28, 1935, Ruth, by

WILSON TO THE RESCUE

When 38-year-old Jimmie Wilson joined the Cincinnati Reds coaching staff in 1939, he accepted that his days as an every-day catcher were behind him. He came to the Reds after five years managing the Phillies, who finished in seventh place three times and eighth (last place) the other two years.

But during the next season, 1940, Willard Hershberger, backup catcher to future Hall of Famer Ernie Lombardi, committed suicide in August. Wilson was asked to replace him. The player-coach appeared in 16 games, batting .243 in 37 at-bats as the Reds tore off toward the NL pennant.

In the World Series, Wilson was called on to suit up and replace an injured Lombardi. Although Wilson had batted just .204 (10 for 49) in his three previous Series appearances, he raked at a .353 clip in the '39 Fall Classic, notching six hits in 17 at-bats. He also scored a pair of runs as Cincinnati beat the Tigers in seven games. Those proved to be Wilson's final at-bats in the Major Leagues.

Wilson

that point playing for the Boston Braves, tracked a deep fly ball hit to left. Ruth, at the tail end of his career, tripped as he reached the incline, and fell on his face.

After collecting himself, Ruth stomped off the field in embarrassment. Just days later, he retired.

CHAPTER 5

PUT A LID ON IT

ASTRODOME

Even before the first fan pushed through the turnstiles in 1965, the new home of the Houston Astros enjoyed a nickname monumental enough to make any Texan proud: The Astrodome was dubbed "The Eighth Wonder of the World."

The multipurpose indoor stadium was the first of its kind. Astros Owner Roy Hofheinz spared no expense in providing for the ballpark's visitors. It was fully air-conditioned and treated 45,000 fans to cloth-covered, padded seats. The Astrodome housed bars and restaurants, as well as a barbershop and — for Hofheinz's personal enjoyment — a bowling alley.

The heat and huge mosquitoes at Colt Stadium — the franchise was known as the Colt .45s before becoming the Astros — caused fans and players alike to welcome the move to a domed ballpark.

Unfortunately, the luxurious facility was not without its own unforeseen issues. Flyballs were hard to track during the day because of the glare of sunlight through the clear roof panels. The panels were eventually painted, but that caused another problem. The lack of sunlight killed the grass. Ultimately, AstroTurf — a nylon synthetic grass surface — was installed. Over the years, AstroTurf would be utilized at 14 Major League fields because it was cheaper to maintain than natural grass.

Opening Day: April 12, 1965
Dimensions: LF: 340 ft.; LF Alley: 375 ft.; CF: 406 ft.; RF Alley: 375 ft.; RF: 340 ft.
First Pitch: Bob Bruce (HOU)
First Home Run: Dick Allen (PHI)
Original Capacity: 42,217
Largest Capacity: 54,816
Also Known As: Harris County Domed Stadium
Cost: $35 Million

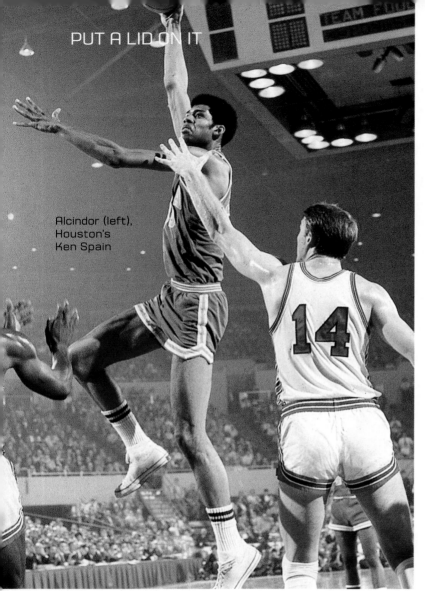

Alcindor (left),
Houston's
Ken Spain

The contest betwee
the University
Houston and UCL
was the first regula
season game broa
cast nationally durir
prime time. It wa
billed "The Game
the Centur

THE GAME OF THE CENTURY

On Jan. 20, 1968, the college basketball world was focused on the Astrodome. The contest between the University of Houston and UCLA was the first regular-season NCAA game to be broadcast nationally on television during prime time. It was billed "The Game of the Century," and pitted the dominant UCLA Bruins, winners of 47 straight games over an almost two-year period, against the Houston Cougars, who had gone undefeated since losing to UCLA in an NCAA semifinal the previous year.

Legendary coach John Wooden's Bruins were ranked No. 1 in the polls and Coach Guy Lewis's Cougars were ranked No. 2. But Houston star Elvin Hayes got the better of UCLA, led by Lew Alcindor (who later changed his name to Kareem Abdul-Jabbar), and snapped the Bruins' long winning streak, 71-69.

BATTLE OF THE SEXES II

Sports fans turned to the Astrodome on Sept. 20, 1973. And it wasn't because the Astros were in a heated pennant race. Tennis took center stage as Bobby Riggs faced Billie Jean King in the "Battle of the Sexes II."

Riggs, a 55-year-old retired tennis star, stirred controversy by publicly belittling women's tennis. After dispatching top player Margaret Court in 1973, Riggs challenged King, a female champ 26 years his junior, whom he labeled the "leading women's libber of tennis."

King had 10 Grand Slam titles on her resume when she stepped onto the court in the Astrodome. She easily won the much-hyped battle in straight sets, 6-4, 6-3, 6-3, silencing Riggs in front of 30,472 fans. At the time it was the largest crowd ever to attend a tennis match.

Riggs (left), King

A CLINCHING NO-HITTER

The Sept. 25, 1986, game at the Astrodome didn't get off to a very good start for Houston right-hander Mike Scott. With his very first pitch, he hit Giants leadoff man Dan Gladden. But Scott adjusted, gained control and started to use his devastating split-fingered fastball to hold San Francisco hitless the rest of the way. His no-hitter took on added importance, as it allowed the Astros to clinch the National League West title over the Cincinnati Reds.

That day, Scott — who would go on to capture the 1986 NL Cy Young Award — became the first pitcher in Major League history to toss a no-hitter in a title-clinching game.

Scott

ROGERS CENTRE

Opening Day: June 5, 1989
Dimensions: LF: 330 ft.; LF Alley: 375 ft.; CF: 400 ft.; RF Alley: 375 ft.; RF: 330 ft.
First Pitch: Jimmy Key (TOR)
First Home Run: Fred McGriff (TOR)
Original Capacity: 50,516
Largest Capacity: 50,598
Also Known As: SkyDome
Cost: $570 Million

When the Toronto Blue Jays set out to design a new ballpark, they wanted the best of both worlds. The franchise wanted the option to play outdoors in the fresh air, but also wanted their field to be protected in the case of inclement weather. The Blue Jays achieved it, revolutionizing stadium construction with a retractable-roof dome. SkyDome, which opened its doors on June 5, 1989, was a state-of-the-art facility. It put to shame the club's previous home, Exhibition Stadium, which was a football venue that had been retrofitted for baseball when the Blue Jays joined the American League 12 years earlier.

The roof at Rogers Centre — the stadium's name was changed from SkyDome in 2005 — features three sliding and rotating panels that are stacked up with a fourth when the roof is open. The 22-million-pound roof takes 20 minutes to open or close. The club's investment, $600 million (Canadian), was worth every penny; the Blue Jays set Major League attendance records as a result, drawing more than 4 million fans each year from 1991 to 1993.

But the roof at the stadium is not its only unique feature. A full-service hotel is connected to the ballpark, allowing fans to sit and take in all the action without leaving the comfort of their rooms. The hotel surrounds the outfield, stretching from foul pole to foul pole.

ROGERS CENTRE'S
11,000-TON ROOF
WEIGHS MORE THAN:

1 EIFFEL TOWER
30 747 JETS
45 STATUES OF LIBERTY
70 BLUE WHALES
850 AFRICAN
ELEPHANTS

OH, CANADA!

When the first World Series took place in 1903, the handful of Big League teams that spread across the Northeast and the Midwest of the United States hardly justified its ambitious moniker. The Fall Classic, though, became a truly international event when it moved outside the United States for the first time in 1992, thanks to the Toronto Blue Jays.

The Jays topped the Oakland A's in the ALCS in 1992 to earn their first World Series berth, and when Toronto hosted the Atlanta Braves on Oct. 20, SkyDome became the site of the first World Series game played outside the U.S. It was a dramatic Series debut, ending in the bottom of the ninth when Toronto's Candy Maldonado snapped a 2-2 tie with an RBI single, giving the Jays a 3-2 walk-off win. Toronto won the next night, too, but was unable to put the Braves away in Game 5, falling, 7-2.

The Jays, though, emerged victorious in a roller-coaster Game 6 in Atlanta. Toronto coughed up a lead in the bottom of the ninth, as the Braves rallied to tie. In the top of the 11th, the Blue Jays scored twice, but it wasn't until Mike Timlin fielded an Otis Nixon bunt and threw him out with a runner at third and two outs that Toronto could celebrate. The 4-3 win brought the Commissioner's Trophy out of the United States for the first time.

JOE CARTER'S DREAM

It's any baseball player's dream — hitting a home run to win the World Series. On Oct. 23, 1993, Joe Carter did just that for the Toronto Blue Jays, knocking a three-run walk-off homer in the bottom of the ninth at SkyDome in the deciding Game 6.

Philadelphia's Mitch "Wild Thing" Williams was called on to preserve a 6-5 Phillies lead and force a Game 7, but he walked Rickey Henderson to lead off the inning. After a flyout, Paul Molitor singled to center. Carter, who was having a mediocre Series, batting just .250, stepped up to the plate with two men on base and one out.

Carter connected on a down-and-in slider, sending a majestic fly ball over the left-field fence for a dramatic 8-6 win and the Jays' second straight world title. It was just the second Series-ending homer, and the first time a come-from-behind walk-off homer had decided a Fall Classic. It also marked the first Series title clinched outside the U.S.

CARTER'S BATTING GLOVES

PUT A LID ON IT

SAFECO FIELD

It was no coincidence that the Seattle franchise started to get serious about building a new home right around the same time that several ceiling tiles fell from the Kingdome's roof in 1994 — fortunately, it happened when the team wasn't playing.

In spite of the decrepit condition of the Mariners' stadium, there was initially serious opposition from local residents to the idea of spending a large amount of public money to build a new ballpark in the franchise's hometown. But after the Mariners got hot late in the 1995 season, surging to the American League West title and a first-round playoff win, the local fans voted to approve funds for an updated facility.

The Mariners moved from the drab Kingdome to sparkling new Safeco Field in 1999. Following the example of the Toronto Blue Jays, Mariners officials wanted to put a roof on the stadium that could be open or closed during games, protecting against the often rainy weather in the Pacific Northwest. The result was a roof that covers nearly nine acres, weighs 22 million pounds and contains enough steel to construct a 55-story skyscraper. It's composed of three movable roof panels, which are powered by 96 10-horsepower electric motors. Because of its extreme size and weight, it takes 10 to 20 minutes to close the roof, with the panels moving from right field across the left-field foul line.

Opening Day: July 15, 1999
Dimensions: LF: 331 ft.; LF Alley: 390 ft.; CF: 405 ft.; RF Alley: 386 ft.; RF: 326 ft.
First Pitch: Jamie Moyer (SEA)
First Home Run: Russ Davis (SEA)
Original Capacity: 46,621
Cost: $517.6 Million

125

Griffey Jr.

'JUNIOR' RETURNS

When he first arrived in Seattle in 1989 he was "The Kid," known for wearing his hat backwards during batting practice, scaling fences for spectacular catches in center field, and clubbing home runs at a record-setting pace. Ken Griffey Jr. was just a teenager when he made his debut with the Mariners. He was an overnight sensation and his rookie-year baseball card was arguably the most coveted object in the country. In 11 seasons playing in the Emerald City, Griffey batted .299 with 398 homers. By the time he was traded to the Cincinnati Reds on Feb. 10, 2000, his popularity was unmatched in the Seattle sports scene.

After moving to the National League, he didn't get the chance to play in Seattle again until June 22, 2007. The 37-year-old Griffey was concerned about how the Seattle crowd would respond to his return. The 13-time All-Star needn't have worried — the fans showered him with ovation upon ovation.

126

ll Pike Place Market, over-
g the Elliot Bay water-
in the northwest corner of
le, is known far and wide for
sh seafood. Tourists come
around the world to see fish-
rs toss three-footers with
But another place in Seattle
ch signature seafood is
he left-field entrance to
o Field. The Ichi-roll — a
tuna roll named after the
rs' outfielder — is available
es.

Ichiro

HIT MACHINE

It didn't take long for Ichiro Suzuki to es-
tablish himself in the Major Leagues after
nine seasons starring for the Orix Blue
Wave in Japan's Pacific League. Ichiro was
the first Japanese position player to make
the jump from Japan's pro ranks to the
Majors when he signed with the Seattle
Mariners prior to the 2001 season.

The Mariners' leadoff man, Ichiro
won the American League batting title in
2001. He earned the Rookie of the Year
Award, and was also voted AL MVP —
joining Boston's Fred Lynn, who pulled off
the double-win in 1975, as the only two
players in history to win both awards in the
same season. His breakout 2001 performance helped the Mariners — who were
supposedly rebuilding after the departure
of superstar shortstop Alex Rodriguez —
to win a division title and tie a Big League
record with 116 regular-season wins.

In his first eight seasons, all spent with
the Mariners, Ichiro racked up at least 200
hits annually, becoming just the second
player in baseball history to accomplish
that. In doing so he tied Willie Keeler's
Major League record for consecutive
200-hit seasons, while establishing a new
AL mark.

Along the way, the slight Ichiro —
standing 5-foot-11 and weighing in at 172
pounds — knocked Hall of Famer George
Sisler out of the record
books after 64 years. Sisler
had held the mark for most
hits in a season with 257 in
1920, but Ichiro collected
262 hits in 2004. Incredibly
adept at simply putting the
ball where the defense was
not, he broke the record on
a simple ground-ball single
up the middle.

SIGNATURE SAFECO FIELD FOOD ITEMS	
FOOD	DESCRIPTION
Salmon Sandwich	Fresh, wild-caught fish served grilled on an organic roll
Garlic Fries	Aromatic, garlic-dusted fries
Ichi-roll	Spicy tuna roll named after Ichiro
Yakisoba Noodles	Stop by *Intentional Wok* to try these fried noodles
Clam Chowder	Fresh chowder from famous Seattle seafood purveyor

PUT A LID ON IT

METRODOME

The Mall of America in suburban Bloomington, Minn., stands on the former site of Metropolitan Stadium which was once home to the Minnesota Twins and the NFL's Vikings. In the mall's amusement park, one can find a plaque commemorating the former location of home plate at the old stadium.

Few tears were shed for the loss of Metropolitan Stadium when it was demolished in 1985. The Twins and Vikings had already abandoned it for a new facility boasting an innovative roof, with air-support technology. The Hubert H. Humphrey Metrodome was constructed with a state-of-the-art fiberglass-fabric ceiling allowing natural light to shine in during the day, while maintaining a comfortable atmosphere for fans when the temperature drops.

Of course, the stadium, known for its "Hefty Bag," which covers the 23-foot right-field wall that hides folded-up seats used for football games, was not without its problems. As with most domes, the roof can give fielders trouble, sometimes causing them to lose sight of the ball against the white cloth background. Adding to the Metrodome's quirks are speakers that hang down from rafters over the field of play. Boston's David Ortiz lost a homer to the speakers in 2006 when a booming drive hit one and fell to the turf in right field. Ortiz, who began his career with the Twins and was quite familiar with the ins and outs of the Metrodome, wound up with just a single.

Opening Day: April 6, 1982
Dimensions: LF: 344 ft.; LF Alley: 385 ft.; CF: 407 ft.; RF Alley: 367 ft.; RF: 327 ft.
First Pitch: Pete Redfern (MIN)
First Home Run: Jim Maler (SEA)
Original Capacity: 54,711
Cost: $68 Million

HOME SWEET DOME

Most baseball teams feel a substantial advantage when they play at their home park. Faithful fans can provide an emotional lift similar to having an extra player on the field or gaining one extra out per inning. This was undoubtedly the case during the 1987 World Series between the Minnesota Twins and the St. Louis Cardinals.

That year, the Series opened with a pair of contests at the Metrodome — the first Fall Classic games ever to be played indoors. With crowds of 55,171 and 55,257, respectively, waving white "homer hankies" and making high-decibel noise in the enclosed facility for their "Twinkies," Minnesota won the first two contests.

But when the Fall Classic shifted to St. Louis, the Cardinals fans were equally loud and supportive of their team. St. Louis captured Games 3, 4 and 5, sending the Fall Classic back to the Metrodome with the Cardinals needing to win just one of two to become world champions.

But Twins fans turned out en masse, took out their "Homer Hankies" once again, and seemed to propel their team to victory. The excitement grew and grew, and the Twins came out the winners in Games 6 and 7 to claim the crown. It was the first time in World Series history that every game had been won by the home team.

Morris

Puckett

1991 WORLD SERIES

The 1991 World Series between the Minnesota Twins and Atlanta Braves was littered with memorable moments.

Minnesota center fielder Kirby Puckett stole the show in Game 6, robbing Ron Gant of a third-inning extra-base hit by climbing Metrodome's left-center field fence. When he came to bat in the 11th, with three hits and two RBI, he launched a 2-and-1 pitch off Charlie Leibrandt for a walk-off homer.

That set the stage in the deciding game for Twins right-hander Jack Morris, who blanked the Braves for 10 innings, allowing just seven hits. Against young John Smoltz, he threw 126 pitches on three days' rest for the second time in the Series. His efforts were rewarded when Gene Larkin's RBI single in the 10th gave the team its second world championship in five years.

Opening Day: April 20, 1912
Dimensions: LF: 324 ft.;
LF Alley: 377 ft.; CF: 458 ft.;
RF: 314 ft.
First Pitch: Buck O'Brien (BOS)
First Home Run:
Hugh Bradley (BOS)
Original Capacity: 35,000
Largest Capacity: 36,984
(day); 37,400 (night)
Cost: $650,000

FENWAY PARK

After moving from the Huntington Avenue Grounds, now part of the Northeastern campus, the Red Sox beat the New York Highlanders (who later became the Yankees) in the first game at their new home, Fenway Park, on April 20, 1912. Although the sinking of the *Titanic* just a few days earlier stole headlines from the stadium's debut, the Red Sox would garner plenty of attention at Fenway Park over the next 90-plus years. Fenway, named after an area of Boston called the Fens, is the oldest stadium in the Major Leagues still in use. Immortalized by author John Updike as a "lyric little bandbox of a ballpark," it's also the smallest, with a capacity below 40,000.

Fenway began to take on its now iconic shape when Owner Thomas A. Yawkey started extensive renovations in 1933, the year he bought the struggling franchise. For the following four decades, Yawkey worked to develop the Boston Red Sox, and oversaw the arrival of players including Jimmie Foxx, Bobby Doerr, Ted Williams, Carl Yastrzemski and Carlton Fisk. As far as the ballpark itself, Yawkey removed "Duffy's Cliff," a 10-foot embankment in front of the left-field fence. Although the area of the park has changed substantially over time, it's now the location of the famous wall, the Green Monster.

THE GREEN MONSTER

At first, it was just a green, 37-foot wall made of concrete and tin, standing in left field. Thomas Yawkey altered the wall partly to prevent fans from watching games for free from a hill beyond the fence.

The wall didn't have a name when it took its present form before the 1934 season. But as time passed, the wall developed a larger-than-life identity. A hand-operated scoreboard was built into it, and remains as one of the last in the Majors. In 1936, a 23-foot net was attached to the top of the wall to keep balls from flying out.

Fans eventually dubbed it the Green Monster, and it has since become the trademark element of Fenway Park. It even serves as the namesake for the Red Sox's mascot — Wally, the Green Monster.

Although its height may have knocked down a few would-be homers over the years, the wall provides an inviting target for singles and doubles that likely would be outs in other parks, especially for righties.

In 2003, owners John Henry, Tom Werner and Larry Lucchino built three rows of seats atop the wall. The new "Monster Seats" have become some of the most sought-after tickets in the league.

Wally, the Green Monster

Yastrzemski

Williams

THE IMPOSSIBLE DREAM

No one expected much from the 1967 Red Sox. During each of the previous seven seasons, they had finished at least 19 games back of the pennant winner in a 10-team league.

But in his first year, Manager Dick Williams ended a "country club" atmosphere in the organization, instilling a sense of urgency and leading his team to a 92-70 record and a first-place finish.

That season, the Red Sox battled Minnesota and Detroit in one of the tightest races ever — a three-team race so close that it wasn't decided until the last day of the regular season. Boston beat the Twins that day and the Tigers split a doubleheader, giving the Sox the division title en route to their first World Series berth since 1946. The season came to be known as "The Impossible Dream."

Although pitcher Jim Lonborg won 22 games and Rico Petrocelli and Tony Conigliaro added a spark, it was Carl Yastrzemski who carried the team. As the race heated up, Yaz batted a sizzling .619 (13 for 21), en route to winning the AL MVP Award. That year, Yastrzemski also became the last player to win the Triple Crown, batting .326 with 44 homers and 121 RBI.

LAST CALL

When Ted Williams came to bat on Sept. 28, 1960, for the final time in his 19-year career, he was 0 for 1 with a walk. Boston scored two in the first inning that day, but by the time Williams batted in the eighth, the club was down, 4-2.

Baltimore's Jack Fisher had replaced starter Steve Barber in the first, and proceeded to shut down Boston. By the eighth, he had allowed just two hits — both singles. But Williams went out in style, blasting a pitch into deep center field for his 521st — and last — home run in the Majors. Boston went on to win the contest, 5-4, scoring twice more in the bottom of the ninth.

Playing his entire career with the Red Sox, Williams finished with a .344 average and a 1.116 OPS, capturing the offensive Triple Crown in 1942 and '47, and the AL MVP Award in 1946 and '49.

FIVE OLDEST BALLPARKS STILL IN USE		
PARK	TEAM	YEAR BUILT
Fenway Park	Boston Red Sox	1912
Wrigley Field	Chicago Cubs	1914
Dodger Stadium	Los Angeles Dodgers	1962
Angels Stadium of Anaheim	Los Angeles Angels of Anaheim	1966
Oakland-Alameda County Coliseum	Oakland Athletics	1966

THE CURSE IS LIFTED!

After the 1919 season, Red Sox Owner Harry Frazee sold several players to the New York Yankees, reportedly to help finance a Broadway musical, "No, No, Nanette." Among them was young pitcher and slugging outfielder, Babe Ruth. The trade would haunt Boston's franchise for nearly nine decades.

Through 1918, the club had won five championships, beginning with the inaugural World Series in 1903. After Frazee sold Ruth, the fortunes of the Red Sox and the Yankees took off in opposite directions.

Boston went 0 for 4 in subsequent World Series appearances, while the Yankees, bolstered by Ruth, embarked on a dynasty that would produce 26 titles in the next 100 years.

Boston's decades-long title drought, which eventually came to be known as "The Curse of the Bambino," was filled with heartbreaking losses. Yankees loyalists taunted Red Sox fans with chants of "19-18, 19-18," reminding them constantly of how long it had been since they had won a championship.

That all changed in 2004. The Red Sox humbled the Yankees in the American League Championship Series, stunning New York by becoming the first team to climb out of a 3-games-to-none hole to win a best-of-seven postseason series. Boston then swept the St. Louis Cardinals in the World Series, putting an end to "The Curse," and to the Red Sox's 86-year dry spell.

Game 1, 2004
World Series

GENUINE S318
Manny Ramirez
2004 WORLD SERIES

Opening Day: April 23, 1914
Dimensions: LF: 327 ft.;
Alley: 390 ft.; CF: 376 ft.;
Alley: 307 ft.; RF: 298 ft.
First Pitch: Claude Hendrix
(Chicago Whales)
First Home Run: Art Wilson
(Chicago Whales)
Original Capacity: 14,000
Largest Capacity: 41,118
Cost: $250,000

WRIGLEY FIELD

Hall of Fame shortstop Ernie Banks called the place "The Friendly Confines." Despite a lack of friendly postseason results, Wrigley Field, the second-oldest Big League park still in use (behind only Boston's Fenway Park), has stood bounded by Clark and Addison streets and Waveland and Sheffield avenues on Chicago's North Side since 1914.

The facility was initially built for the Federal League's Chicago Whales, but the Cubs moved in two years later, naming the stadium after owner William Wrigley Jr. in 1926. The Cubs drew 1 million fans during the 1927 season, the first NL team to do so.

The park's lively atmosphere extends well beyond its ivy-covered walls, into the surrounding neighborhood, dubbed "Wrigleyville," where fans can watch games from stands erected on the rooftops of buildings across the street. When the sometimes-formidable wind is blowing out toward Lake Michigan, pop-ups can turn into home runs, leading to high-scoring games and souvenirs for fans waiting outside the outfield wall for launched balls. But when the wind is blowing in off of the lake, Wrigley becomes a pitcher's park.

The field has become famous for, among other things, its 27-by-75-foot hand-operated scoreboard behind the center-field bleachers, and the flags in center field. The flags still alert local residents as to whether the Cubs have won or lost a game.

THE HOLY HOUSES

Hartnett (center)

HOMER IN THE GLOAMIN'

It was the greatest homer that no one saw. Gabby Hartnett's home run at Wrigley Field on Sept. 28, 1938, left the Pirates in the dark and propelled the Cubs to the National League pennant.

When the Pirates came to Wrigley for a three-game series on Sept. 27, they were 1.5 games ahead of Chicago. But the Cubs won the opener, slicing Pittsburgh's lead to just a half-game.

It was tied, 5-5, heading into the ninth. With no lights at Wrigley, darkness was creeping in, but the umpires said there would be one more inning. The Pirates couldn't score, and the first two Cubs went down in order in the bottom of the ninth.

By the time Hartnett, Chicago's player-manager, came to the plate, darkness had enveloped Wrigley. The count went to 0 and 2, but Hartnett crushed the next pitch, sending the ball flying into the bleachers in left-center field and giving the Cubs a 6-5 win.

It took a while for cheers to fill Wrigley, as few fans could track the path of the ball in the dark sky. They heard the crack of contact, but it wasn't until the ball landed among fans in left-center, prompting them to begin cheering, that everyone knew Hartnett had hit what became known as the "Homer in the Gloamin'."

The win pushed Chicago to a half-game lead over the Pirates in the standings. Chicago swept that series and ultimately captured the National League pennant.

IVY-COVERED WALLS

Wrigley Field's most famous feature, the ivy that covers the outfield wall, actually hasn't been there since the beginning. Bill Veeck, whose father had been the club's president until his death in 1933, planted it in 1937.

Veeck planted 350 Japanese bittersweet plants to fill the space while 200 Boston ivy plants took root. His plan worked perfectly, but as the vines flourished, they became a bit of an

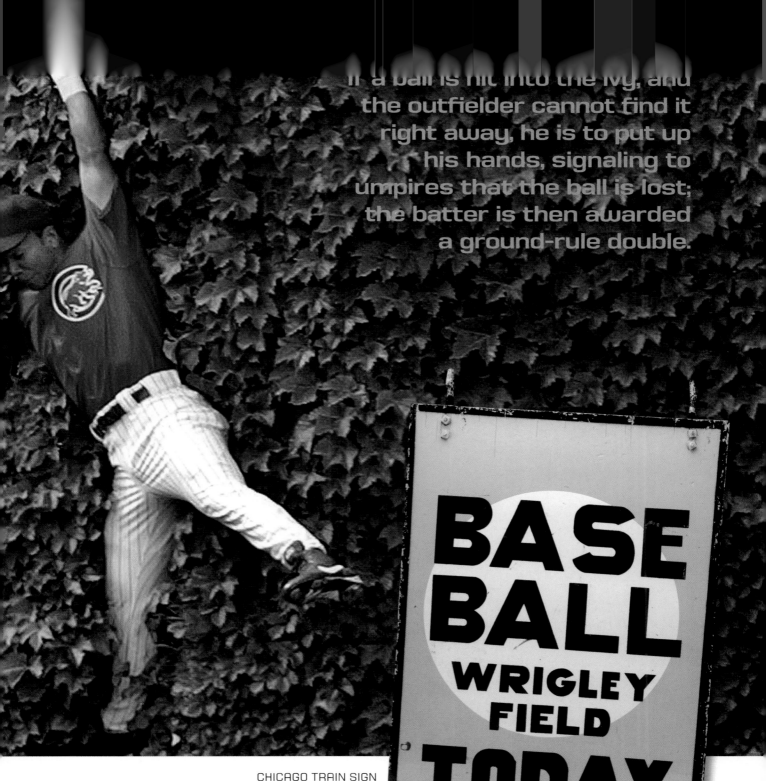

If a ball is hit into the ivy, and the outfielder cannot find it right away, he is to put up his hands, signaling to umpires that the ball is lost; the batter is then awarded a ground-rule double.

BASE BALL WRIGLEY FIELD TODAY

CHICAGO TRAIN SIGN

issue for outfielders chasing balls that rolled to the wall. Sometimes players would reach down and pull up leaves instead of baseballs.

As a result of the dense outfield foliage, Wrigley Field was forced to develop some unique ground rules. If a ball is hit into the ivy and the outfielder can't find it right away, he is to put up his hands, signaling to umpires that the ball is lost. In that case, the batter is awarded a ground-rule double.

But fielders at Wrigley must think quickly. If an outfielder attempts to make a play on a ball that has become caught in the ivy-covered wall, it's then considered to be in play. In that case, runners are entitled to take as many bases as they can while the fielder searches.

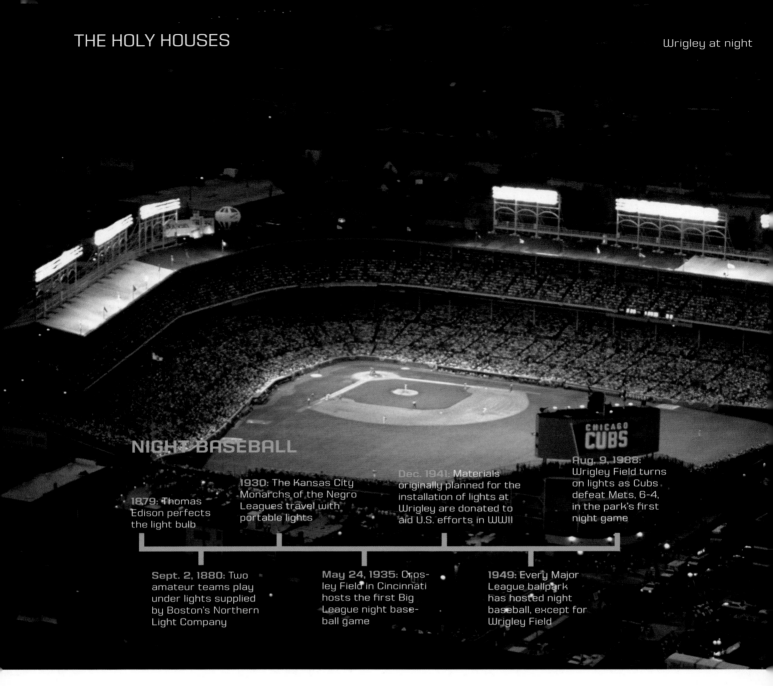

NIGHT BASEBALL

1879: Thomas Edison perfects the light bulb

1930: The Kansas City Monarchs of the Negro Leagues travel with portable lights

Dec. 1941: Materials originally planned for the installation of lights at Wrigley are donated to aid U.S. efforts in WWII

Aug. 9, 1988: Wrigley Field turns on lights as Cubs defeat Mets, 6-4, in the park's first night game

Sept. 2, 1880: Two amateur teams play under lights supplied by Boston's Northern Light Company

May 24, 1935: Crosley Field in Cincinnati hosts the first Big League night baseball game

1949: Every Major League ballpark has hosted night baseball, except for Wrigley Field

LET THERE BE LIGHT

Although Wrigley Field was the last ballpark in the Major Leagues to install lights for night baseball games, the franchise was actually scheduled to make the addition in 1942. Cubs Owner Philip K. Wrigley, however, decided to donate the lights to a shipyard the day after the attack on Pearl Harbor.

So the Cubs kept on playing baseball during the day at Wrigley Field until Major League Baseball executives told club officials in 1984 that if they made the postseason tournament and didn't have a facility that could accommodate a night game for television purposes, those games would have to be moved to a park that did have lights.

In the Cubs' residential location on the north side of Chicago, the stadium's neighbors weren't too keen on the idea of megawatt light bulbs keeping them up late at night, and it created a thorny political issue. But on Feb. 23, 1988, the Cubs finally forged ahead with the plans, and the neighborhood's residents grudgingly consented. The first regular-season game to be played at night was scheduled for Aug. 8, 1988. After four innings, though, rain forced them to stop that game against the Phillies. The first full game under the lights was played the next day, against the New York Mets. Under the bright lights and in front of a raucous Wrigley crowd, the Cubs defeated the Mets, 6-4.

Sam Sianis, nephew of William and owner of the Billy Goat Tavern, with pet goat

THE BILLY GOAT HEX

All William Sianis wanted to do was watch Game 4 of the 1945 World Series at Wrigley Field — with his goat.

As the story goes, Sianis bought two seats, one for himself and one for his billy goat. Ushers confronted him and he explained that there was no disclaimer saying he couldn't use the ticket for the goat. The pair was permitted to sit, but not for long. Cubs Owner Philip K. Wrigley had them removed due to the goat's odor.

Sianis did not take kindly to being kicked out. He claimed to have placed a curse on the Cubs, guaranteeing that they would never again reach the World Series.

Chicago lost that Series, dropping Game 7 at home, and hadn't been back to the Fall Classic for more than 60 years, leading many to believe in "the Billy Goat Hex."

Fueling such beliefs was the Cubs' September collapse in 1969 and the ground ball through Leon Durham's legs in the 1984 NLCS. Of course there was also the foul ball caught by a fan in 2003, which led to a Florida Marlins comeback when Chicago was just five outs away from the Series.

TIGER STADIUM

The site of Tiger Stadium, at the corner of Michigan and Trumbull avenues in the city of Detroit, was steeped in baseball history from the very beginning.

After Bennett Park, the club's previous home, was demolished in 1911, the Tigers built a new fire-proof steel-and-concrete structure on the same site. Their new home, originally called Navin Field, opened on April 20, 1912, the same day Boston's Fenway Park made its debut. After later going by Briggs Stadium for many years, the ball-park finally came to be known as Tiger Stadium in 1961.

Owner Walter O. Briggs under-took a renovation in 1936, giving the ballpark its trademark right-field porch — a covered second deck extending out over the lower deck and 10 feet out over the field. It was an inviting home run target, especially for left-handed hitters. Another landmark stood on the grass in center field — a 125-foot flagpole that was in play, nearly 440 feet from home plate.

While renovations commissioned by Briggs increased capacity from 23,000 to 54,500 in 1937, the fa-cility had very little foul territory, allowing fans to feel like they were on top of the action.

Tiger Stadium, which also played host to the NFL's Lions from 1938 to 1974, was the site of three Major League All-Star Games, as well as the Tigers' World Series triumphs in 1968 and 1984. The stadium was partially demolished in 2008.

Opening Day: April 20, 1912
Dimensions: LF: 345 ft.; LF
Alley: 365 ft.; CF: 467 ft.; RF
Alley: 370 ft.; RF: 370 ft.
First Pitch:
George Mullin (DET)
First Home Run:
Del Pratt (STL Browns)
Original Capacity: 23,000
Largest Capacity: 54,220
Also Known As: Navin
Field, Briggs Stadium
Cost: $300,000

McLain

Lolich

McLAIN, LOLICH AND THE 1968 TITLE

The one-two punch of pitchers Denny McLain and Mickey Lolich sparked the Tigers to a 1968 World Series win over the Cardinals.

McLain was a dominant force for Detroit during the regular season, finishing with a 31-6 record and a 1.96 ERA, and earning the Cy Young Award. He also contributed one win against St. Louis in the World Series. But it was paunchy left-hander Mickey Lolich who was the postseason ace for the Tigers. Lolich, no slouch during the regular season (going 17-9), won three games against the Cardinals in the Fall Classic.

Lolich allowed just five earned runs in 27 innings, and put up three complete-game wins, earning Series MVP honors. He won Game 2, came back on three days rest for a Game 5 win, and after just two days of recovery, polished off the Cards, out-dueling St. Louis ace Bob Gibson for a 4-1 triumph in the deciding Game 7.

THE BIRD

He talked to the baseball. He smoothed the dirt on the mound. People started calling him "Big Bird" because he looked a lot like the *Sesame Street* character.

Out of nowhere, animated Tigers right-hander Mark Fidrych became a national phenomenon in 1976, packing the stands for his starts both at home and on the road. Attendance at Tiger Stadium during his 18 home starts that year accounted for nearly half of the team's 81-game total. Opposing teams even asked the Tigers to rearrange their rotation so he could pitch in their parks.

Fidrych, who made the team out of Spring Training as a non-roster invitee, won 19 games and led the league in ERA (2.34) and complete games (24). At 21, Fidrych was the starting AL pitcher in the All-Star Game, en route to winning Rookie of the Year honors, earning just the Major League-minimum $19,000.

It wasn't just his pitching that drew attention. It was how he told the ball where to go before winding up. It was the way he strutted on the mound after outs.

Unfortunately, Fidrych's peak lasted just a season. Torn cartilage in his knee and an undiagnosed torn rotator cuff limited him to 11 starts in 1977. He made just 16 more Big League starts through 1980 before calling it a career in 1983.

Fidrych

MARK FIDRYCH

DETROIT TIGERS

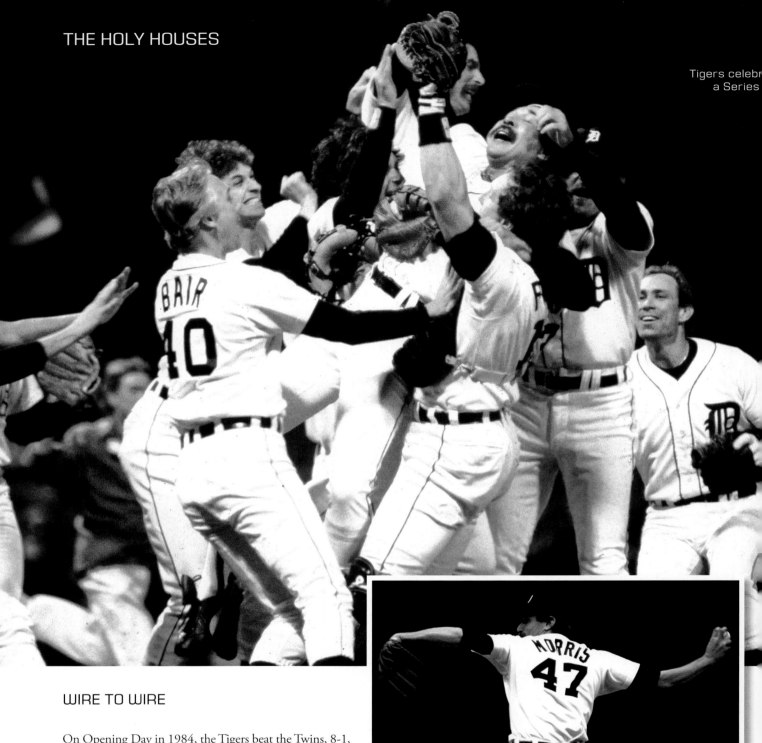

Tigers celebr
a Series

WIRE TO WIRE

On Opening Day in 1984, the Tigers beat the Twins, 8-1, in Minnesota. So when the next day's papers showed the Tigers on top of the AL East at 1-0, it wasn't a shock.

But they never relinquished that top spot. The Tigers roared out to an amazing 26-4 record, eclipsing the 1955 Dodgers' mark (25-5) for the best 30-game start in Major League history. And the team kept rolling, running its record to an astounding 35-5, the best 40-game mark ever. Finishing with a club-record 104 wins, Detroit was led by hurlers Dan Petry and Jack Morris (who tossed a no-no on April 7), and received offensive contributions up and down the line-up, notably from Kirk Gibson, Alan Trammell and Lou Whitaker.

They clinched the division title on Sept. 18, with a 3-0 win over Milwaukee in front of 48,810 fans. By the end of the season, they had shattered the franchise's previous attendance record, drawing 2,704,794 fans to Tiger Stadium in 1984.

Not only did the '84 Tigers stay in first place from wire to wire, but they also swept Kansas City in the ALCS and disposed of the San Diego Padres in five games to win the World Series. It was one of the most dominant seasons by any team in history.

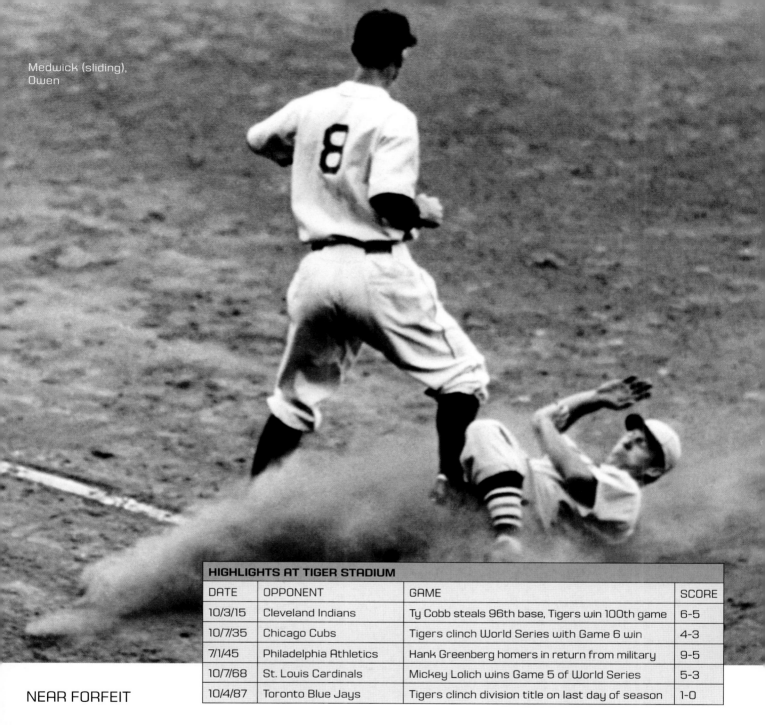

Medwick (sliding), Owen

HIGHLIGHTS AT TIGER STADIUM

DATE	OPPONENT	GAME	SCORE
10/3/15	Cleveland Indians	Ty Cobb steals 96th base, Tigers win 100th game	6-5
10/7/35	Chicago Cubs	Tigers clinch World Series with Game 6 win	4-3
7/1/45	Philadelphia Athletics	Hank Greenberg homers in return from military	9-5
10/7/68	St. Louis Cardinals	Mickey Lolich wins Game 5 of World Series	5-3
10/4/87	Toronto Blue Jays	Tigers clinch division title on last day of season	1-0

NEAR FORFEIT

The 1934 World Series had been a back-and-forth affair, and the Detroit Tigers and St. Louis "Gashouse Gang" Cardinals found themselves facing off in a make-or-break Game 7 for the world title.

The problems began in the sixth inning, when St. Louis took a 9-0 lead at Tiger Stadium. With two outs, the Cardinals' Joe Medwick tripled and slid hard into third baseman Marv Owen. A squabble ensued.

Heading out to the field in the bottom of the inning, Medwick was greeted with empty bottles, fruit and other debris. Detroit's angry fans — clearly upset by his behavior and the score — nearly caused the Cardinals to walk off the field, which would have forced the Tigers to forfeit. To quash the problem, Commissioner Kenesaw Mountain Landis had Medwick removed from the game.

It wasn't a popular decision with the Cardinals, but he came out anyway. In the end, neither the incident nor Medwick's removal affected the outcome of the game. St. Louis won, 11-0, and claimed its third world championship in five years.

YANKEE STADIUM

By 1922, the Yankees had been sharing the Polo Grounds with the New York Giants for 10 seasons. Since 1920, Babe Ruth had been rocketing homer after homer over the fence in right field and the Giants, increasingly irritated that the Yankees outdrew them on a regular basis — mostly a result of Ruth — asked them to move.

So they did. The Yankees built their own ballpark in the Bronx. Yankee Stadium, complete with its own short porch in right field made to cater to the Babe, opened on April 18, 1923. The Bambino won the stadium's debut game, 4-1, against his former team, the Boston Red Sox, with a three-run shot before a crowd of 74,200. Such Herculean displays led fans from all over to call Yankee Stadium, "The House That Ruth Built."

Yankee Stadium's trademark was a white copper frieze along the upper deck, 108 feet above the field. The original field was known for short lengths down the lines and for a monstrous outfield area called "Death Valley."

Before the 1974 season, Yankees Owner George Steinbrenner ordered renovations, forcing the team to spend two years at Shea Stadium in Queens. But the legend of Yankee Stadium kept on growing after the club returned in 1976, through moments like Reggie Jackson's three-homer game in the 1977 World Series, and Aaron Boone's 11th-inning walk-off homer in Game 7 of the 2003 ALCS.

Opening Day: April 18, 1923
Dimensions: LF: 255 ft.; LF Alley: 474 ft.; CF: 487 ft.; RF Alley: 423 ft.; RF: 255 ft.
First Pitch: Bob Shawkey (NYY)
First Home Run: Babe Ruth (NYY)
Original Capacity: 58,000
Largest Capacity: 82,000
Cost: $2.5 Million

THE HOLY HOUSES

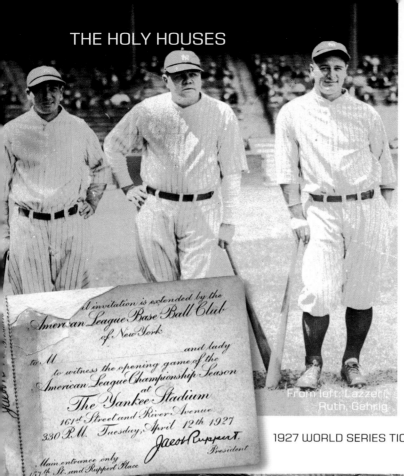

From left: Lazzeri, Ruth, Gehrig

1927 WORLD SERIES TICKET

MURDERERS' ROW

Picking the best all-time Yankees era is no easy task. Not for an organization that racked up 26 world titles during its years at Yankee Stadium after building it in 1923. But one group manages to stand out: The powerful 1927 lineup that earned the moniker of the "Murderers' Row."

In his eighth year with New York in 1927, Babe Ruth set a historic home run standard, launching a Big League record 60 longballs — a mark that would go unmatched until Roger Maris broke it in 1961. That season, Ruth knocked in 164 runs and batted .356 with a .772 slugging percentage.

Lou Gehrig, a 24-year-old first baseman, smashed 47 homers in 1927, with 175 RBI and a .373 average, en route to a 17-season career with the Yankees. All together, the team hit a record-breaking 158 homers that year and scored 975 runs, most of the power coming from Ruth, Gehrig, Bob Meusel and Tony Lazzeri. With a 110-44 record, the Yankees took the AL pennant by 19 games.

MONUMENT PARK

Originally located in deep center field, Monument Park, which honored special individuals from the Yankees' organization, was moved behind the fence when the ballpark was renovated in the 1970s.

Manager Miller Huggins, who died in 1929, was the first to be honored with a monument. Lou Gehrig and Babe Ruth were the next to be honored. Monuments were later dedicated to Mickey Mantle and Joe DiMaggio. In 2001, those who lost their lives on 9/11 were honored as well. Owner Jacob Ruppert, who was responsible for building Yankee Stadium, was the first to be honored with a plaque, in 1940. Others who have been similarly honored include Thurman Munson, Roger Maris, Whitey Ford, Billy Martin, announcer Mel Allen and public address announcer Bob Sheppard.

RETIRED YANKEES NUMBERS	
NO.	PLAYER
1	Billy Martin
3	Babe Ruth
4	Lou Gehrig
5	Joe DiMaggio
7	Mickey Mantle
8	Yogi Berra, Bill Dickey
9	Roger Maris
10	Phil Rizzuto
15	Thurman Munson
16	Whitey Ford
23	Don Mattingly
32	Elston Howard
37	Casey Stengel
42	Jackie Robinson*
44	Reggie Jackson
49	Ron Guidry

*ceremonious

Gehrig

THE LUCKIEST MAN

Yankees first baseman Lou Gehrig was forced into early retirement by amyotrophic lateral sclerosis (ALS), a progressive neurodegenerative disease that affects nerve cells in the brain and spinal cord. On July 4, 1939, he was honored on the field at Yankee Stadium. Initially too emotional to speak, Gehrig gathered strength and stepped to the microphone.

"Fans, for the past two weeks, you have been reading about a bad break I got," said Gehrig. "Yet today I consider myself the luckiest man on the face of the earth."

Gehrig played in 2,130 consecutive games before bowing out. His talent and stamina earned him the nickname "The Iron Horse," and made his early retirement all the more devastating.

Gehrig passed away on June 2, 1941, just more than two weeks shy of his 38th birthday. ALS has commonly become known as "Lou Gehrig's Disease."

Jeter

2001 WORLD SERIES

With the country reeling from the Sept. 11, 2001, terrorist attacks that demolished the Twin Towers at the World Trade Center, the Yankees provided New Yorkers a brief distraction by staging two of the most improbable comebacks in World Series history. After edging the Diamondbacks, 2-1, in Game 3, the Yankees showed their flair for the dramatic over the next two games.

In Game 4, New York erased a two-run deficit in the bottom of the ninth with a single by Paul O'Neill and a game-tying homer by Tino Martinez. Both hits came with two outs against Arizona's Byung-Hyun Kim. Derek Jeter won the game with a walk-off solo shot in the 10th inning, knotting the Series at two games apiece.

There were more heroics in Game 5, this time from Scott Brosius, who blasted a two-out, two-run homer off Kim in the bottom on the ninth, tying the game, 2-2. The Yankees would win, 3-2, on an RBI single by Alfonso Soriano in the 12th.

The Yankees were unable to win the world championship, though. The Diamondbacks pulled off a two-run, ninth-inning rally of their own in Game 7, capturing the title on a Luis Gonzalez bloop single off Mariano Rivera.

Pope Benedict XVI

MORE THAN BASEBALL

Yankee Stadium has served as the venue for far more than just historic baseball events. Home of the New York Football Giants from 1956 to 1973, the Stadium was the site for the NFL title game on Dec. 28, 1958, dubbed "The Greatest Game Ever Played." The Colts tied that game with a field goal with seven seconds left and beat the Giants in overtime, 23-17. In addition, the ballpark staged college football games, notably the 1928 affair between Army and Notre Dame. It was at halftime of that game that Notre Dame coach Knute Rockne gave his "win one for the Gipper" speech, in reference to former All-American halfback George Gipp, who had passed away in 1920.

It wasn't uncommon for championship prizefights to be held in Yankee Stadium, either. The most legendary of these bouts occurred on June 22, 1938, when Joe Louis knocked out reigning world heavyweight champ Max Schmeling in the first round in one of eight title fights that Louis fought in the Stadium.

Yankee Stadium also was the site of three Papal visits. Pope Paul VI conducted a mass on Oct. 4, 1965, and Pope John Paul II on Oct. 2, 1979. On April 20, 2008, Pope Benedict XVI celebrated mass at "The House That Ruth Built."

FAREWELL

On April 18, 1923, the Bronx Bombers opened Yankee Stadium with a win over the Boston Red Sox. And they closed the ballpark with a win, too, downing Baltimore, 7-3. Yankee Stadium hosted its final game on Sept. 21, 2008, closing its doors after 85 seasons to make way for a new home across the street.

The ballpark was rich with festivities before the final game, with numerous stars from the past and present paying tribute to the Stadium and its history. Babe Ruth's daughter, 92-year-old Julia Ruth Stevens, threw out the ceremonial first pitch. After the game, team captain Derek Jeter addressed the fans, thanking them for their support.

"There's a lot of tradition, a lot of history, a lot of memories," Jeter said of Yankee Stadium. "We want to have you take the memories of this field, add them to the new memories that will come at the new Yankee Stadium and pass them along from generation to generation."

Then Jeter, along with his teammates and other Yankees legends, took one last lap around Yankee Stadium, one of the most historic sports arenas in history.

Jeter

SOURCE NOTES

INTRODUCTION

6. "To Hoboken, Baseball Began Here," Sullivan, Joseph F. *New York Times* 20 June 1990.

7. Pastier, John; *Historic Ballparks*, Chartwell Books, Inc., Edison, N.J., 2006; pp 65, 67, 97.

CHAPTER 1

9. Pastier, John; *Historic Ballparks*, Chartwell Books, Inc., Edison, N.J., 2006; pp 65, 67, 97.

9. Baltimore Orioles 2008 media guide; pp 414–415.

9. www.ballparksofbaseball.com

10. Pastier, John; *Historic Ballparks*, Chartwell Books, Inc., Edison, N.J., 2006, pp 26, 59.

11. "Best Signature Ballpark Food and Hot Dogs;" Pahigian, Josh and O'Connell, Kevin; special to ESPN SportsTravel; www.sports.espn.go.com 10 July 2007.

13. "I think the time is right" Associated Press; www.sportsillustrated.cnn.com 20 Sept. 1998.

13. "Chronology of Ripken's Streak" Reuters; www.sportsillustrated.cnn.com 20 Sept. 1998.

13. "With Graces, Ripken Becomes a Legend," Maske, Mark. *Washington Post* 7 Sept. 1995.

13. "American Baseball Legend Babe Ruth;" Gollust, Shelley; www.voanews.com 1 April 2006.

13. www.baberuthmuseum.com

13. www.entertainment.howstuffworks.com

14. Pastier, John; *Historic Ballparks*, Chartwell Books, Inc., Edison, N.J., 2006; pp 64–65.

14. www.ballparksofbaseball.com

14. Cleveland Indians 2008 media guide; pp 26–31.

16. Cleveland Indians 2008 media guide; pp 448–468.

16. Krasner, Steven; *Pedro Martinez*, Chelsea House Publishers, Philadelphia, 2005.

16. "No new-school drummer boy" www.cleveland.indians.mlb.com 19 July 2006.

16. "Talking tech with Cleveland's ballpark drummer" McNamara, Paul. www.networkworld.com 15 April 2008.

16. "Heart of Indians Baseball Beats From the Cheap Seats" Caldwell, Dave. www.nytimes.com 9 Sept. 2007.

18. "Indians sellout streak ends at 455" www.cbc.ca 4 April 2001.

18. Cleveland Indians 2008 media guide; pp 32.

18. "A Tribute To an All-Star Grandmother," Anderson, Dave. www.nytimes.com 9 July 1997.

18. "All-Star Results – 1997" www.mlb.com 8 July 1997.

21. www.ballparksofbaseball.com

21. Pastier, John; *Historic Ballparks*, Chartwell Books, Inc., Edison, N.J., 2006; pp 134–137.

21. www.baseball-almanac.com

23. Colorado Rockies 2008 media guide; pp 424–425.

23. www.baseball-reference.com

24. www.baseball-almanac.com

24. "Hideo No-No: Nomo No-Hits Rockies at Coors" Brown, Tim. Los Angeles *Daily News*. www.highbeam.com 18 Sept. 1996.

24. "For pitchers, Coors Field humidor is nirvana" Stone, Larry. *Seattle Times* 27 Oct. 2007.

24. "Rockies idea of fair play: Put baseballs in humidor" Michaelis, Vicki. *USA Today* 10 Oct. 2007.

24. "Big winning streak puts Rockies in rare air" Dodd, Mike. *USA Today* 16 Oct. 2007.

26-27. Pastier, John; *Historic Ballparks*, Chartwell Books, Inc., Edison, N.J., 2006; pp 49–50, 66, 80.

26–27. www.ballparksofbaseball.com

28. "How George W. Bush Scored Big With the Texas Rangers" Lewis, Charles. www.angelfire.com 18 Jan. 2000.

28. "A series of beneficial moves" Farrey, Tom. www.espn.com 1 Nov. 2007.

29. Texas Rangers 2008 media guide; page 259.

29. Detroit Tigers 2007 media guide; pp 182–183.

29. New York Yankees 2008 media guide; pp 250–251.

29. www.baseball-reference.com

31. www.baseball-almanac.com

31. "Rogers Throws Perfect Game for Rangers" Associated Press 29 July 1994.

31. Texas Rangers 2008 media guide; pp 374–375.

33. www.ballparks.com

33. www.thefieldfinder.com

33. www.cwsomaha.com

CHAPTER 2

35. Pastier, John; *Historic Ballparks*, Chartwell Books, Inc., Edison, N.J., 2006; pp 30–31, 34, 181.

35. www.ballparksofbaseball.com

36. "Robinson's debut flew under the national radar" Becker, Jim. Associated Press; www.nbcsports.msnbc.com 13 April 2007.

36. www.baseball-almanac.com

36–37. www.everything2.com

36–37. Kahn, Roger; *The Boys of Summer*. Harper Perennial, May 2006.

38. www.streetplay.com

38. Golenbock, Peter; *Bums: An Oral History of the Brooklyn Dodgers*. Putnam Pub Group, 1984.

38. "Dem Brooklyn Bums Go West" Bryk, William. www.nypress.com 2008.

38. Los Angeles Dodgers media guide; pp 404.

39. www.sportsencyclopedia.com

39. "Tense Political Vote preceded Dodgers' Move West 50 Years Ago" Felde, Kitty. www.scpr.org 22 July 2008.

40. www.ballparksofbaseball.com

40. Pastier, John; *Historic Ballparks*, Chartwell Books, Inc., Edison, N.J., 2006; pp 44, 152–155.

40. Los Angeles Dodgers 2008 media guide; pp 420–421.

42. www.radiohof.org

42. Los Angeles Dodgers 2008 media guide; pp 510–511.

43. www.baseballhalloffame.org

43. www.thebaseballpage.com

43. www.baseballhistorian.com

43. www.jewishvirtuallibrary.org

44. "A hobbled Gibson homers in a pinch (or, 'Clutch Kirk,' Part II)" MLB.com Baseball's Best www.mlb.com 15 Oct. 1988.

44. www.baseball-almanac.com

45. "25 Years After Fernandomania" Martin, Jorge. *Dodger Magazine* 18 Aug. 2006.

45. www.baseballlibrary.com

45. Los Angeles Dodgers 2008 media guide; pp 517–518.

47. Pastier, John; *Historic Ballparks*, Chartwell Books, Inc., Edison, N.J., 2006; pp 13, 27, 37, 181–185.

47. www.ballparksofbaseball.com

47. www.andrewclem.com

49. "The Shot Heard Round the World" Ray, James Lincoln. www.baseballsuite101.com 28 Feb. 2008.

49. "Thomson hits the shot heard 'round the world" Lowitt, Bruce. www.sptimes.com 18 Dec. 1999.

49. "The Goof That Changed the Game" Olbermann, Keith. www.sportsillustrated.cnn.com 23 Sept. 2008.

49. "Fred Merkle and the 1908 Giants" www.members.aol.com 26 Sept. 2008.

51. 1954 World Series. www.worldseries.com

51. "The Catch' is still The Play" Stark, Jayson. www.espn.com 3 May 2007.

51. www.baseball-reference.com

52. Pastier, John; *Historic Ballparks*, Chartwell Books, Inc., Edison, N.J., 2006; pp 13, 27, 37, 181–185.

52. www.ballparksofbaseball.com

52. San Francisco Giants 2008 media guide; pp 434–435.

54. www.sanfrancisco.giants.mlb.com

54. San Francisco Giants 2008 media guide; pp 438.

56. 2002 World Series. www.worldseries.com

56. www.baseball-almanac.com

56. "Ichiro's inside job leads to another AL victory" www.mlb.com 10 July 2007.

56. "Bonds moves into eternity, assumes MLB home run record" Associated Press 8 Aug. 2007.

CHAPTER 3

58–60. Pastier, John; *Historic Ballparks*, Chartwell Books, Inc., Edison, N.J., 2006; pp 23, 208–213, 216.

58–60. www.ballparksofbaseball.com

60. www.baseballlibrary.com

61. 1909 World Series. www.worldseries.com

61. www.clpgh.org

61. www.baseball-almanac.com

62. "Babe Ruth's Final Home Run" *Pittsburgh Post Gazette* 11 July 2006.

62. www.ballparks.com

63. Krasner, Steven; *Play Ball Like the Hall of Famers*, Peachtree Publishers, Atlanta, Ga., 2005; pp 111–112.

63. "In 1960, a Series to Remember (or Forget)" Hamill, Sean D. *New York Times* 24 June 2008.

63. "Pirates win, 10-9, Capturing Series on Homer in 9th" Drebinger, John, Special to the NY Times, www.select.nytimes.com

64. Pastier, John; *Historic Ballparks*, Chartwell Books, Inc., Edison, N.J., 2006; pp 211.

64. www.ballparksofbaseball.com

64. Pittsburgh Pirates 2008 media guide; pp 354–355.

66. "Ward launches first homer into Allegheny" Associated Press, *USA Today* 7 July 2002.

66–67. www.ballparksofbaseball.com

68. "Primanti Bros. Sandwiches" Kinsman, Kat. www.slashfood.com 8 Sept. 2007.

68. "The Primanti Tradition" Bradish, Kelly. PittsburghLIVE www.pittsburghlive.com 9 Dec. 2002.

69. www.latinosportslegends.com

69. "Pittsburgh's Clemente Bridge is first to get a lighting sponsor" Bucsko, Mike. *Pittsburgh Post-Gazette* 28 Nov. 2001.

69. "Roberto Clemente Bridge (Sixth Street Bridge)" www.tripadvisor.com

71. Pastier, John; *Historic Ballparks*, Chartwell Books, Inc., Edison, N.J., 2006; pp 44, 148–149.

71. www.ballparksofbaseball.com

72–73. "Kansas City Monarchs" Negro Leagues Baseball Museum, www.coe.ksu.edu

72–73. Satchel Paige Biography, www.satchelpaige.com

72–73. www.baseball-almanac.com

73. www.ballparktour.com

73. Kansas City Sports Teams History Museum, www.home.kc.rr.com

73. www.ballparkdigest.com

75. Pastier, John; *Historic Ballparks*, Chartwell Books, Inc., Edison, N.J., 2006; pp 56–57, 148–151.

75. www.ballparksofbaseball.com

75. Kansas City Royals media guide, 2008, pp 8-9.

76. "Latest Dates Above .400 Since 1980" Krasnow, Lonny. www.sportsillustrated.cnn.com

76. www.thebaseballpage.com

77. "May 15, 1973: Nolan Ryan throws his first no-hitter" Ramos, Ricardo. www.angelswinblog.blogspot.com 10 March 2008.

77. "This Day in History 1973: Nolan Ryan pitches first no-hitter" www.history.com 15 May 1973.

78. 1985 World Series: "Bad Call Gives Royals New Life" www.mlb.com

79. www.kansascity.royals.mlb.com

80. Pastier, John; *Historic Ballparks*, Chartwell Books, Inc., Edison, N.J., 2006; pp 13, 18, 25, 236–240.

80. www.ballparksofbaseball.com

82–83. www.baseballlibrary.com

82–83. www.baseball-reference.com

82-83. www.stan-the-man.com

83. "Game 7 of the 1946 World Series: Cardinals vs. Red Sox Final Highlighted By Enos Slaughter's Mad Dash" Ray, James Lincoln. www.baseball.suite101.com 18 Oct. 2008.

83. "100 Years of the World Series: The Mad Dash, 1946, Game 7" www.time.com 2003.

83. "Country's Mad Dash wins it for St. Louis" Lowitt, Bruce. *St. Petersburg Times* 4 Oct. 1999.

84. 1944 World Series. www.worldseries.com

85. "Baseball's Smallest Player Ever" Ray, James Lincoln. www.baseball.suite101.com 31 May 2007.

85. "Short on size, long on history" Rovell, Darren. www.espn.go.com 16 Aug. 2007.

86. Pastier, John; *Historic Ballparks*, Chartwell Books, Inc., Edison, N.J., 2006; pp 49–50, 236–241.

86. www.ballparksofbaseball.com

88. "Jack Buck, 77, Measured Voice of Cardinals Baseball" Sandomir, Richard. *New York Times* 19 June 2002.

88. www.baseballvoices.com

88. "Coleman Bites the Tarp" Chen, Hogan and Lyons, Alexis. Flashbacks www.baseballlibrary.com 2002.

88. "Man-eating tarp is bankroll away" *San Diego Union-Tribune* 27 July 2005.

89. St. Louis Cardinals 2008 media guide; pp 454–455.

89. www.hickoksports.com

89. "Top Moments in Cardinals NLCS History" Kiley, Gabe. www.insidestl.com 10 Oct. 2008.

89. www.historicbaseball.com

89. St. Louis Cardinals 2008 media guide; pp 438–439.

90–91. www.baseballlibrary.com

90–91. www.baseball-reference.com

90–91. St. Louis Cardinals 2008 media guide; pp 428.

CHAPTER 4

93. Pastier, John; *Historic Ballparks*, Chartwell Books, Inc., Edison, N.J., 2006; pp 22–23, 200–205.

93. www.ballparksofbaseball.com

95. www.baseball-almanac.com

95. www.bucketfoot.com

95. "Connie Mack Biography: Philadelphia Athletics Hall of Fame Baseball Manager" Rowland, Michael. www.americanhistory.suite101.com 31 Jan. 2008.

95. www.thebaseballpage.com

96. Pastier, John; *Historic Ballparks*, Chartwell Books, Inc., Edison, N.J., 2006; pp 25–26, 108–113.

96. www.ballparksofbaseball.com

98. "Thank Caray, Chicago for Popularity of 'Take Me Out to the Ballgame'" Drehs, Wayne. www.sports.espn.go.com 8 July 2008.

98. www.radiohof.org

98. www.baseballhalloffame.org

99. "A Game of Their Own" Enders, Eric. *Major League Baseball All-Star Game Program*, 2000.

99. www.negroleaguebaseball.com

100. Pastier, John; *Historic Ballparks*, Chartwell Books, Inc., Edison, N.J., 2006; pp 26–27, 248–250.

100. www.ballparksofbaseball.com

102. "Mantle's 'Washington Wallop' Gave Birth to Tape-Measure Homer" Pitoniak, Scott. www.baseballhalloffame.org 15 Feb. 2007.

102. "Chuch Stobbs; served up the longest home run in history; 79" Schudel, Matt. *The Washington Post* 28 July, 2008.

103. "Greatest World Series Moments" www.bucketfoot.com

103. "A World Series for Baseball's Greatest Pitcher" Hornestay, David. www.major-league-baseball.suite101.com 24 Sept. 2007.

103. www.cmgww.com

105. Pastier, John; *Historic Ballparks*, Chartwell Books, Inc., Edison, N.J., 2006; pp 13–14.

105. www.ballparks.com

106–107. www.mlb.mlb.com

106–107. www.baseballlibrary.com

106–107. www.entertainment.howstuffworks.com

107. "The First Baseball Game of the 20th Century" Enders, Eric. www.ericenders.com *New York Times* 3 April 2000.

109. Pastier, John; *Historic Ballparks*, Chartwell Books, Inc., Edison, N.J., 2006; pp 32–33, 37.

109. www.ballparksofbaseball.com

109. www.ballparks.com

110. www.baseball-almanac.com

110–111. www.diamondfans.com

110–111. "Hall of Fame, 82, won 363 games" Associated Press, www.espn.go.com 25 Nov. 2003.

112. Pastier, John; *Historic Ballparks*, Chartwell Books, Inc., Edison, N.J., 2006; pp 26, 28, 116–118.

112. www.ballparksofbaseball.com

114–115. www.baseball-statistics.com

115. www.baseball-reference.com

115. www.baseball-almanac.com

CHAPTER 5

116. Pastier, John; *Historic Ballparks*, Chartwell Books, Inc., Edison, N.J., 2006; pp 26, 51–52, 144–146.

116. www.ballparksofbaseball.com

116. Houston Astros 2008 media guide; pp 280.

118. "Battle of the sexes" Holden, Anthony. www.cbs.sportsline.com 20 Sept. 1973.

118. "King defeats Riggs in Battle of the Sexes II" www.history.com 20 Sept. 1973.

118. "The Game of the Century: Looking back 40 years" Gonzales, J.R. www.blogs.chron.com 20 Jan. 2008.

118. "Game of the Century" Norwood, Robyn. Los Angeles Times www.latimesblogs.latimes.com 20 Jan. 2008.

119. "Five most memorable Astros games" Hoffman, Jared. *The Sporting News*, www.sportingnews.com 1999.

119. "An Interview with Mike Scott" Kerby, Ray. www.astrosdaily.com 4 Feb. 2002.

120. Pastier, John; *Historic Ballparks*, Chartwell Books, Inc., Edison, N.J., 2006; pp 55–56, 58, 244–247.

120. www.ballparksofbaseball.com

120. Toronto Blue Jays 2008 media guide; pp 474–475.

122. 1992 World Series, www.mlb.com 24 Oct. 1992.

122. Toronto Blue Jays 2008 media guide; pp 269–274.

123. Toronto Blue Jays 2008 media guide; pp 269–274.

123. 100 Years of the World Series www.time.com 2003.

123. www.baseball-almanac.com

123. 1993 World Series/Game 6 www.mlb.com 23 Oct. 1993.

125. Pastier, John; *Historic Ballparks*, Chartwell Books, Inc., Edison, N.J., 2006; pp 65–66, 230, 232–235.

125. www.ballparksofbaseball.com

125. www.ballparktour.com

127. Seattle Mariners 2008 media guide; pp 133–140.

127. "MVP caps Ichiro's dream season" Hickey, John. *Seattle Post-Intelligencer* 21 Nov. 2001.

127. "Ichiro passes Sisler, pads record" Associated Press www.sports.espn.go.com 2 Oct. 2004.

129. Pastier, John; *Historic Ballparks*, Chartwell Books, Inc., Edison, N.J., 2006; pp 55, 166–173.

129. www.ballparksofbaseball.com

129. Minnesota Twins 2008 media guide; pp 408–409.

130. www.baseball-almanac.com

130. "Twins announce return of Homer Hanky" www.twins.mlb.com 26 Sept. 2003.

130–131. Minnesota Twins media guide, pp 303–320.

131. "1991 World Series had it all" Caple, Jim. Special to ESPN.com www.espn.go.com 19 Nov. 2003.

CHAPTER 6

133. Pastier, John; *Historic Ballparks*, Chartwell Books, Inc., Edison, N.J., 2006; pp 19, 27-28, 100–105.

133. www.ballparksofbaseball.com

133. Boston Red Sox 2008 media guide; pp 41–46.

134. Boswell, John; Fisher, David; *Fenway Park: A Stadium Pop-Up Book*, Little, Brown and Company, Boston, 1992.

135. "Sox honor 'Impossible Dream' team" McPhillips, Alex. www.mlb.com 10 April 2007.

135. Reynolds, Bill; *Lost Summer: The '67 Red Sox and the Impossible Dream*, Warner Books, New York, N.Y., 1992.

135. "Hub Fans Bid Kid Adieu" Updike, John. *The New Yorker* 22 Oct. 1960.

135. www.baseball-almanac.com

135. www.history.com

136. Shaughnessy, Dan; *Reversing the Curse: Inside the 2004 Boston Red Sox*, Houghton Mifflin Company, Boston/New York, 2005.

139. Pastier, John; *Historic Ballparks*, Chartwell Books, Inc., Edison, N.J., 2006; pp 18, 23, 32, 108–112.

139. www.ballparksofbaseball.com

139. Chicago Cubs 2008 media guide; pp 362–364.

140. www.ballparks.com

140. www.robertedwardauctions.com

140–141. www.baseball-reference.com

140–141. www.ballparks.com

142. "The Cubs get lights at Wrigley Field" Vettel, Phil. *Chicago Tribune* 8 Aug. 1988.

142. www.mlb.mlb.com

143. "Da Curse of the Billy Goat Timeline" www.dacurse.com

143. "Chicago Cubs' Legendary Curses" Ray, James Lincoln. www.baseball.suite101.com 2 July 2007.

144. Pastier, John; *Historic Ballparks*, Chartwell Books, Inc., Edison, N.J., 2006; pp 28, 30, 138–143.

144. www.ballparksofbaseball.com

146. Detroit Tigers 2008 media guide; pp 358.

146. www.thebaseballpage.com

146. www.baseball-alamanac.com

146. www.detroit-tigers-baseball-history.com

147. " 'Bird' Fidrych was workhorse in '76" Bodley, Hal. *USA Today* 10 Aug. 2006.

147. "One strange bird: Mark Fidrych" Hakwins, Jim. *The Sporting News* 22 July 1999.

148. www.baseball-reference.com

148. www.baseballlibrary.com

149. www.baseball-almanac.com

150. Pastier, John; *Historic Ballparks*, Chartwell Books, Inc., Edison, N.J., 2006; pp 36–39, 41, 66, 181, 183-191.

150. www.ballparksofbaseball.com

150. New York Yankees 2008 media guide; pp 14–17.

152. www.montgomerycollege.edu

152. www.bestsyndication.com

152. New York Yankees 2008 media guide; pp 19–21.

152. "Monument Park" Begley, Ian. www.dailynews.com 2007.

153. "Lou Gehrig bids farewell to baseball" Smith, Paul C. www.mlb.com 23 July 2002.

153. www.lougehrig.com

153. Robinson, Ray and Jennison, Christopher; *Yankee Stadium: Drama, Glamor, and Glory*, Viking Studio, New York, N.Y., 1998, pp 54–55.

154. www.baseball-almanac.com

154. New York Yankees 2008 media guide; pp 27.

154. Durso, Joseph; *Yankee Stadium: Fifty Years of Drama*, Houghton Mifflin Company, Boston, 1972, pp 125–150.

155. "Jeter address capped Yankee Stadium sendoff" Edes, Gordon. *Yahoo! Sports* 22 Sept. 2008.

155. "A Long Goodbye to an 85-Year Run" Kepner, Tyler. *New York Times* 21 Sept. 2008.

155. "Legends make last curtain call at Yankee Stadium" Feinsand, Mark; Yaniv, Oren; Hutchinson, Bill. *Daily News* 22 Sept. 2008.

CREDITS

CORBIS: 92 (Shibe park)

BOB GOMEL//TIME LIFE PICTURES/GETTY IMAGES: 82 (Musial)

BRAD MANGIN/MLB PHOTOS: 52 (AT&T Park); 132 (Fenway Park)

BRAD MANGIN/SPORTS ILLUSTRATED/GETTY IMAGES: 54 (Kayaker)

BRIAN BAHR/GETTY IMAGES: 22 (Home Run)

DAVE ARRIGO/MLB PHOTOS: 68 (Primanti Bros.)

DAVID E. SCHERMAN/TIME & LIFE PICTURES/ GETTY IMAGES: 34 (Ebbets Field)

DIAMOND IMAGES/GETTY IMAGES: 13 (Ruth Statue); 115 (Wilson)

DOUG PENSINGER/ALLSPORT: 29 (I. Rodriguez); 32 (Rosenblatt)

ELSA/GETTY IMAGES: 86 (Busch Stadium II)

ERIC MILLER/GETTY IMAGES: 128 (Metrodome)

EZRA O. SHAW: 144 (Tiger Stadium)

FOCUS ON SPORT/GETTY IMAGES: 118 (Battle of the Sexes); 130 ('87 WS); 135 (Yastrzemski)

GEORGE ROSE/GETTY IMAGES: 42 (Scully)

HARRY HOW/GETTY IMAGES: 120 (Rogers Centre)

HY PESKIN/TIME LIFE PICTURES/GETTY IMAGES: 85 (Gaedel); 110 (Feller)

JAMES DRAKE/SPORTS ILLUSTRATED/GETTY IMAGES: 43 (Koufax)

JAMIE SQUIRE/GETTY IMAGES: 69 (Roberto Clemente Bridge)

JED JACOBSOHN/GETTY IMAGES: 25 (Colorado WS); 54 (McCovey Cove); 55 (Kayakers)

JEFF GROSS/GETTY IMAGES: 56 (Suzuki)

JERRY DRIENDL/GETTY IMAGES: 10 (Camden Yards, 2)

JIM McISAAC/GETTY IMAGES: 134 (Wally); 152 (Monument Park, 2)

JOHN BRYSON//TIME LIFE PICTURES/GETTY IMAGES: 39 (Moving West)

JOHN FROSCHAUER /ICON SMI/CORBIS: 126 (Griffey Jr.)

JOHN IACONO/SPORTS ILLUSTRATED/GETTY IMAGES: 44 (Gibson)

JOHN ZICH/AFP/GETTY IMAGES: 140 (Ivy)

JOHN ZICH/NEWSPORT/CORBIS: 143 (Sianis, Billy Goat)

JONATHAN DANIEL/GETTY IMAGES: 138 (Wrigley Field)

JOSEPH SOHM/VISIONS OF AMERICA/CORBIS: 31 (Inside Arlington)

JUDY GRIESEDIECK//TIME LIFE PICTURES/ GETTY IMAGES: 128 (Metrodome top)

JULIE JACOBSON/AFP/GETTY IMAGES: 154 (Pope)

KIDWILER COLLECTION/DIAMOND IMAGES/ GETTY IMAGES: 146 (McLain)

KIMBERLY BARTH/AFP/GETTY IMAGES: 19 (Alomar Jr.)

LEONARD MCCOMBE/TIME LIFE PICTURES/ GETTY IMAGES: 95 (Mack)

LOUIS REQUENA/MLB PHOTOS: 69 (Clemente)

MLB PHOTOS: 8 (Camden Yards); 14 (Progressive Field); 18 (Progressive Sellout Game); 24 (Nomo); 27 (Rangers close-up); 32 (Lamade); 50 (Mays); 64 (PNC Park); 66 (PNC Aeriel); 74 (Kauffman Stadium); 88 (Buck); 89 (Gibson); 111 (Spahn/Sain); 131 (Morris)

MARK RUCKER/TRANSCENDENTAL GRAPH-ICS/GETTY IMAGES: 51 (Ruth); 62 (Ruth); 70 (Municipal Stadium); 72 (Monarchs); 79 (O'Neil); 108 (Braves Field); 116 (Astrodome)

MARK E. GIBSON/CORBIS: 66 (Allegheny River)

MICHAEL ZAGARIS/MLB PHOTOS: 16 (Indians)

MIKE POWELL/GETTY IMAGES: 45 (Valenzuela)

NBLA/MLB PHOTOS: 36 (Robinson); 58 (Forbes Field); 60 (Forbes Field); 61 (Cobb); 83 (Slaughter); 94 ('29 WS); 99 (East-West Game); 106 (South End Grounds); 107 (1900 Opener); 112 (Crosley Field); 135 (Williams); 140 (Hartnett)

OTTO GREULE JR/GETTY IMAGES: 29 (Gonzalez, 2); 124 (Safeco Field); 127 (Suzuki)

PAUL JASIENSKI/GETTY IMAGES: 20 (Coors Field)

PETER NEWCOMB/AFP/GETTY IMAGES: 90 (Scoreboard)

RICH CLARKSON/SPORTS ILLUSTRATED/ GETTY IMAGES: 118 (Basketball)

RICH PILLING/MLB PHOTOS: 24 (Humidor); 76 (Brett); 122 ('92 WS); 148 ('84 WS)

RICK STEWART/GETTY IMAGES: 123 (Carter)

RONALD MARTINEZ/GETTY IMAGES: 26 (Rangers Ballpark); 29 (A. Rodriguez); 31 (Arlington, 2)

RONALD C. MODRA/SPORTS ILLUSTRATED/ GETTY IMAGES: 78 ('85 Controversy); 142 (Night Game)

RONALD C. MODRA/SPORTS IMAGERY/GETTY IMAGES: 148 (Morris)

RON VESELY/MLB PHOTOS: 56 ('02 WS); 131 (Puckett); 136 ('04 WS); 154 ('01 WS)

ROB TRINGALI/SPORTSCHROME/GETTY IM-AGES: 134 (Green Monster)

ROBERT BECK/SPORTS ILLUSTRATED/GETTY IMAGES: 57 (Bonds)

TODD OLSZEWSKI/MLB PHOTOS: 11 (BBQ)

TONY TOMSIC/MLB PHOTOS: 147 (Fidrych)

UNDERWOOD & UNDERWOOD/CORBIS: 80 (Sportsman's Park)

WALTER IOOSS JR./SPORTS ILLUSTRATED/ GETTY IMAGES: 12 (Ripken)

INDEX

Aaron, Hank, 57

Abdul-Jabbar, Kareem, 118

Adams, John, 17

Alcindor, Lew, 118

Allegheny River, 58, 66, 69

Allen, Dick, 116

Allen, Mel, 152

Alomar, Roberto, 17, 77

Alomar, Sandy Jr., 16, 19

Alomar, Sandy, Sr., 77

Anderson, Dave, 44

Andujar, Joaquin, 78

Angels Stadium of Anaheim, 136

Anthony, Eric, 15

Arizona Diamondbacks, 25, 154

Army, 154

Astrodome, 116–119

Astroturf, 75, 86, 88, 116

AT&T Park, 6, 52–57

Atlanta Braves, 122, 131

B&O Warehouse, 9, 10, 11

Babe Ruth Museum, 13

Bacsik, Mike, 57

Baerga, Carlos, 16

Balboni, Steve, 78

Ball, Philip DeCatesby, 85

Baltimore & Ohio Railroad, 10

Baltimore Colts, 154

Baltimore Orioles, 8, 9, 11, 12, 13, 155

Banks, Ernie, 72, 139

Barber, Red, 42

Barber, Steve, 135

Battle of the Sexes II, 118

Bell, James "Cool Papa," 72

Belle, Albert, 16

Bench, Johnny, 112

Bennett Park, 144

Berkman, Lance, 11

Berra, Yogi, 152

"Big Bird," 147

Big Red Machine, 25

"Billy Goat Hex," 143

Bishop, Max, 95

Blake, John, 95

Blanchard, Johnny, 63

Bleacher Bums, 38

Blues Stadium 71, 73

Boley, Joe, 95

Bonds, Barry, 53, 54, 56, 57, 90, 92

Boone, Aaron, 150

Boston Beaneaters, 105, 107

Boston Braves, 37, 62, 105–111, 115

Boston Post, 110

Boston Red Sox, 13, 17, 18, 25, 37, 51, 83, 86, 89, 105, 106, 109, 132–137, 150, 155

Boston University, 109

Boudreau, Lou, 110

Bouquet Street, 62

Boys of Summer, 36, 37

Branca, Ralph, 49

Braves Field, 108–111

Brett, George, 76

Bridwell, Al, 49

Briggs, Walter O., 144

Brock, Lou, 86

Brogna, Rico, 20

Bronx Bombers, 155

Brooklyn Dodgers, 34–39, 49, 83, 107 also see Los Angeles Dodgers

Brosius, Scott, 154

Brown, Willard, 72

Browning, Tom, 30

Bruce, Bob, 116

Buck, Jack, 45, 88

Busch, August, 80

Busch Stadium, 80, 85 also see Sportsman's Park

Busch Stadium II, 80, 85–91

Bush, George W., President of the United States, 28

California Angels, 12, 30, 56, 77 also see Los Angeles Angels of Anaheim

Camden Yards, 8–13, 31 also see Oriole Park at Camden Yards

Campanella, Roy, 37

Candlestick Park, 52

Caray, Harry, 98

Carter, Joe, 123

Casey, Sean, 64

Charleston, Oscar, 99

"Charley O." 73 also see Finley, Charley O.

Chavez Ravine, 40

Chester, Hilda, 7, 38

Chicago Cubs, 43, 49, 79, 97, 136, 38–143, 149

Chicago Defender, 99

Chicago Tribune, 99

Chicago Whales, 139

Chicago White Sox, 77, 96–98

China Basin, 52, 55

Cincinnati Reds, 25, 89, 106, 112–115, 119, 126

Clark, Jack, 78

Clemente, Roberto, 58, 64, 69

Cleveland Indians, 14–19, 50, 110, 149

Cleveland Municipal Stadium, 14

Cobb, Ty, 61, 149

Coleman, Vince, 88

Colorado Rockies, 20–25

Colt Stadium, 116

Columbia Park, 93

Comiskey, Charles, 96

Comiskey Park, 31, 96–99

Conigliaro, Tony, 135

Connor, Roger, 47

Coors Canaveral, 23

Coors Field, 20–25

Court, Margaret, 118
Crosley Field, 112–115, 142
 also see Redland Field
Culberson, Leon, 83
"Curse of the Bambino," 136
Davis, Mike, 44
Davis, Zachary Taylor, 96
Denkinger, Don, 78
Detroit Tigers, 61, 85, 89, 115, 135,
 144–149
Dickey, Bill, 152
DiMaggio, Joe, 152
Dodger Stadium, 40–45, 136
Doerr, Bobby, 133
Dreyfuss, Barney, 58
Drysdale, Don, 43
"Duffy's Cliff," 133
Dunn, Jack, 13
Durham, Leon, 143
Dykes, Jimmy, 95
East-West Game, 99
Ebbets, Charles, 35, 40
Ebbets Field, 7, 31, 34–39, 42, 83
Eckersley, Dennis, 44, 45
Edison, Thomas, 142
Eighth Wonder of the World, 116
Elster, Kevin, 53
Elysian Fields, 6
Elysian Hills, 40
Erskine, Carl, 37
Estes, Shawn, 19
Eutaw Street, 11
Evers, Johnny, 49
Exhibition Stadium, 120
Exposition Park, 58, 64, 66, 67
Faust, Nancy, 98
Federal League, 139
Feller, Bob, 110
Fenway Park, 6, 10, 18, 31, 64, 106,
 111, 132–137, 139, 144
Fernandomania, 45
Fidrych, Mark, 7, 147
Fielder, Prince, 54
Finley, Charlie O., 73
 also see "Charley O"
Fisher, Jack, 135
Fisk, Carlton, 133
Flatbush, 35, 36, 40
Florida Marlins, 25, 143
Forbes Field, 10, 58–63, 96
Ford, Whitey, 152
Foster, Bill, 99
Foxx, Jimmie, 95, 133
Frazee, Harry, 136
Freeman, Buck, 107
"Friendly Confines," 139
 also see Wrigley Field
Gaedel, Eddie, 85
Gant, Ron, 131
Gateway Arch, 86–87
Gehrig, Lou 9, 12, 152, 153
Gibson, Bob, 86, 89, 146
Gibson, Josh, 99
Gibson, Kirk, 44–45, 148
Gipp, George, 154
Gladden, Dan, 119
Gonzalez, Juan, 29

Gonzalez, Luis, 154
Gonzalez, Mike, 83
Gowdy, Hank, 103
"Grand Pavillion," 105
Greenberg, Hank, 60, 149
Green Monster, 31, 133, 134
Greer, Rusty, 30
Grieve, Ben, 11
Griffey, Ken, Jr., 126
 also see "The Kid"
Griffith, Clark, 100
Griffith Stadium, 7, 100–103
Guidry, Ron, 152
Haas, Mule, 95
Hall, Bill, 86
Hargrove, Mike, 16
Harris, Bucky, 103
Hart, John, 16
Hartnett, Gabby, 140
Hayes, Elvin, 118
Hedges, Robert Lee, 85
"Hefty Bag," 129
Henderson, Rickey, 123
Henry, John, 134
Hern, Gerald, 110
Hershberger, Willard, 115
Hershiser, Orel, 42
Hodges, Gil, 37
Hodges, Russ, 49
Hofheinz, Roy, 116
Holliday, Matt, 20
Holmes, Tommy, 110
"Homer Hankies", 130
"Homer in the Gloamin'," 140
Houston Astros, 66, 116–119
Hovley, Steve, 77
Howard, Elston, 72, 152
Howard, Frank, 59
Hubert H. Humphrey Metrodome,
 128–131
 also see Metrodome
Hudler, Rex, 30
Huggins, Miller, 152
Humidor, 23, 24
Hunt, Lamar, 73
Huntington Avenue Grounds,
 105, 133
Iorg, Dane, 78
Ivy, 140–141
Jacobs Field, 14
 also see Progressive Field
Jackson, Bo, 75
Jackson, Reggie, 150, 152
Jackson, Travis, 103
Japan's Pacific League, 127
Jeter, Derek, 154–155
Johnson, Arnold, 71
Johnson, Davey, 12
Johnson, Randy, 30
Johnson, Walter, 103
 also see "The Big Train"
"Jury Box", 109
Kahn, Roger, 37
Kansas City Athletics, 71, 73
Kansas City Blues, 71, 73
Kansas City Chiefs, 73
Kansas City Cowboys, 73

Kansas City Monarchs, 36, 71–73, 79,
 99, 142
Kansas City Royals, 34, 71, 73,
 74–79, 148
Kansas City Spurs, 73
Kauffman, Ewing, 73, 75
Kauffman Stadium, 73, 74–79
Keeler, Willie, 127
Key, Jimmy, 120
Kim, Byung-Hyun, 154
Kiner, Ralph, 58, 59, 60, 61
King, Billie Jean, 118
Kingdome, 125
Klinger, Bob, 83
Koufax, Sandy, 42, 43
Labine, Clem, 37
Lajba, John, 33
Lamade Stadium, 32–33
Landis, Commissioner Kenesaw
 Mountain, 149
Larkin, Gene, 131
Lasorda, Tommy, 44
Lavagetto, Cookie, 37
Lazzeri, Tony, 152
Leibrandt, Charlie, 131
Lewis, Darren, 17
Lewis, Guy, 118
Lindstrom, Freddy, 103
Little League World Series, 32–33
LoDo District, 21
Lofton, Kenny, 16
Lolich, Mickey, 89, 146, 149
Lombardi, Ernie, 115
Lonborg, Jim, 135
Los Angeles Angels of Anaheim, 136
 also see California Angels
Los Angeles Dodgers, 40–45, 89, 91,
 136, 148
 also see Brooklyn Dodgers
Los Angeles Memorial Coliseum, 40
"Lou Gehrig's Disease", 153
Louis, Joe, 154
Lucchino, Larry, 134
Lynn, Fred, 127
Mack, Connie, 7, 93–95, 107
Maldonado, Candy, 122
Maler, Jim, 129
Mall of America, 129
Malone, Pat, 95
Mantle, Mickey, 7, 102, 152
Marichal, Juan, 112
Maris, Roger, 90, 152
Martin, Billy, 152
Martinez, Dennis, 15
Martinez, Pedro, 17
Martinez, Tino, 154
Masi, Phil, 110
Mattingly, Don, 152
May, Lee, 122
Mayberry, John, 75
Mays, Willie, 50, 52
Mazeroski, Bill, 63
McCormick, Mike, 110
McCovey Cove, 54, 55
McCovey, Willie, 54, 55
McGriff, Fred, 120
McGwire, Mark, 90–91

McLain, Denny, 146
McNeely, Earl, 103
Medwick, Joe, 149
Mendez, Jose, 72
Meoli, Rudy, 77
Merkle, Fred, 49
Metrodome, 129–131
 also see Hubert H. Humphrey
 Metrodome
Metropolitan Stadium, 129
Meusel, Bob, 152
Mile High Stadium, 21
Miller, Bing, 97
Milwaukee Brewers, 85
Minnesota Twins, 129–131, 135, 148
"Miracle" Braves, 106, 107, 110
"Mistake by the Lake," 14
Molitor, Paul, 123
Monongahela River, 58
"Monster Seats," 134
Montreal Expos, 89
Monument Park, 152
Morgan, Joe, 79
Morris, Jack, 131, 148
Moyer, Jamie, 125
Muehlebach Field, 71, 73
Muehlebach, George, 71, 73
Mulder, Mark, 86
Municipal Stadium, 7, 70–75
Munson, Thurman, 152
Murderers' Row, 152
Murray, Eddie, 16
Musial, Stan "The Man," 82–83
Navin Field, 144
NCAA College Division I World
 Series, 32–33
Negro American League, 36, 73
Negro Leagues Baseball Museum, 79
Negro National League, 99
Nehf, Art, 95
Newcombe, Don, 37, 49
New York Football Giants, 154
New York Giants, 37, 47–51, 103, 106
New York Highlanders, 133
New York Mets, 75, 77, 89, 142
New York Yankees, 37, 51, 56, 63, 71,
 136, 150–155
Nickerson Field, 109
Niedenfuer, Tom, 89
Nilsson, Dave, 27
Nixon, Otis, 122
Nomo, Hideo, 24
Notre Dame, 154
Oakland-Alameda County Coliseum,
 136
Oakland Athletics, 44–45, 56, 98,
 122, 136
O'Day, Hank, 49
Omaha Municipal Stadium, 32
O'Malley, Walter, 39–40
O'Neil, John "Buck," 72, 79
O'Neill, Paul, 11, 154
Orta, Jorge, 78
Oriole Park at Camden Yards, 8–13
 also see Camden Yards
Orix Blue Wave, 127
Orth, Al, 107

Ortiz, David, 11, 129
Otis, Amos, 75, 77
Ott, Mel, 47
Owen, Marv, 149
Pacific Bell Park, 56
Paige, Leroy "Satchel," 72–73
Palace of the Fans, 112
Patek, Freddie, 77
Patterson, Red, 102
Pena, Alejandro, 44
Pena, Tony, 16
Pesky, Johnny, 83
Petrocelli, Rico, 135
Petry, Dan, 148
Philadelphia Athletics, 71, 92–95,
    107, 149
Philadelphia Phillies, 25, 76, 107,
    115, 123, 142
Piazza, Mike, 20
Pinson, Vada, 77
Pittsburgh Courier, 99
Pittsburgh Crawfords, 99
Pittsburgh Pirates, 37, 58–61,
    63–69, 140
Plank, Eddie, 92–93
PNC Park, 7, 58, 64-69
Podres, John, 37, 41
Polo Grounds, 6, 46–51, 150
Pope Benedict XVI, 154
Pope John Paul II, 154
Pope Paul VI, 154
Post, Wally, 41, 112
Powell, Boog, 11
Primanti Brothers Sandwiches, 7, 68
Progressive Field, 14-19
    also see Jacobs Field
Puckett, Kirby, 131
Pulliam, Henry, 49
Ramirez, Manny, 16, 42
Rangers Ballpark in Arlington,
    26–31
Redfern, Pete, 129
Redland Field, 112–115
    also see Crosley Field
Reese, Pee Wee, 37
Richmond, Lee, 30
Riggs, Bobby, 118
Ripken, Cal Jr., 9, 12
Ritchie, Todd, 64
Rivera, Mariano, 154
Rizzuto, Phil, 152
Robinson Field, 85

Robinson, Jackie, 36–37, 39, 72,
    99, 152
Rockne, Knute, 154
Rodriguez, Alex, 29, 125, 127
Rodriguez, Henry, 11
Rodriguez, Ivan, 19, 29
Rodriguez, Rich, 54
Rogan, Wilber, 72
Rogers Centre, 120–123
    also see SkyDome
Rogers, Kenny, 27, 30
Root, Charlie, 95
Rosenblatt, Johnny, 33
Rosenblatt Stadium, 32–33
Royals Stadium, 73
Ruel, Muddy, 103
Rueter, Kirk, 53
Ruppert, Jacob, 152
Ruppert Stadium, 73
Ruth, George Herman, 13, 51, 57,
    62, 99, 114–115, 136, 150, 152,
    155, 157
Ryan, Nolan, 77
Safeco Field, 124–127
Sain, Johnny, 110–111
St. Louis Browns, 80, 84–85
St. Louis Cardinals, 78, 80–91, 98,
    130, 136, 146, 149
St. Mary's Industrial School for Boys, 13
Saberhagen, Bret, 78
Salkeld, Bill, 110
San Diego Padres, 148
San Francisco Chronicle, 103
San Francisco Giants, 52–57, 112 119
San Gabriel Mountains, 40
Schmeling, Max, 154
Schoendienst, Red, 86
Scott, Mike, 119
Scully, Vin, 42
Seattle Mariners, 124–127
Sesame Street, 147
Shea Stadium, 75, 150
Sheppard, Bob, 152
Shibe, Ben, 93
Shibe Park, 7, 10, 93–95, 96
Sianis, William, 143
Simmons, Al, 95
Sisler, George, 127
SkyDome, 120–123
    also see Rogers Centre
Slaughter, Enos "Country", 83, 86
Smith, Hal, 53

Smith, Hilton, 72
Smith, Ozzie, 88–89
Smoltz, John, 131
Snider, Duke, 37
Soriano, Alfonso, 154
Sorrento, Paul, 9, 16, 27
Sosa, Sammy, 64, 90
South End Grounds, 104–107
Spahn, Warren, 110–111
Spain, Ken, 118
Sparrow, Roy, 99
"Spite fence," 93
"Splash" hits, 54–55
Splitorff, Paul, 75
Sportsman's Park, 80-85
    also see Busch Stadium
Stanky, Eddie, 110
Stargell, Willie "Pops," 41, 68
Steinbrenner, George, 150
Stengel, Casey, 152
Stevens, Julia Ruth, 155
Stevens, Lee, 11
Stewart, Bill, 110
Stobbs, Chuck, 102
"Sun Deck," 112
Sutcliffe, Rick, 9
Suzuki, Ichiro, 56, 127
Swift, Billy, 20
Sym-Phony Band, 38
Taft, Pres. William Howard, 100
"Take Me Out to the Ballgame," 98
Tanner, Chuck, 98
"Tape-Measure Homer," 102
Terry, Ralph, 63
Texas Rangers, 26–31
"The Big Train," 103
    also see Johnson, Walter
"The Catch," 50
"The Game of the Century," 118
"The Greatest Game Ever Played," 154
"The House That Ruth Built," 51,
    150, 154
    also see Yankee Stadium
"The Impossible Dream," 135
"The Kid," 126
    also see Griffey, Ken Jr.
"The Terrace," 114–115
Thome, Jim, 9, 11, 15, 16
Thomson Bobby, 48–49
Three Rivers Stadium, 58, 64
Tiger Stadium, 7, 31, 144–149
Timlin, Mike, 122

Titanic, 133
Toronto Blue Jays, 120-123, 125, 149
Trachsel, Steve, 92
Trammell, Alan, 148
Tudor, John, 78
University of California, Los Angeles,
    118
Uggla, Dan, 86
University of Houston, 118
Updike, John, 133
Valenzuela, Fernando, 45
Vander Meer, Johnny, 35
Vaughn, Mo, 11
Veeck, Bill, 85, 96, 140
Vizquel, Omar, 16
Von der Ahe, Chris, 80
Waddell, Rube, 93
Wagner, Honus, 47, 61, 67
Walker, Harry, 83
Walker, Larry, 23
Wally, The Green Monster, 134
Walsh, Ed, 97
Ward, Daryle, 66
Washington Nationals, 57
Washington Senators, 100–103
Weaver, Earl, 12
Webster, Cody, 33
Wells, David, 30
Wells, Kip, 66
Werner, Tom, 134
Wertz, Vic, 50
Whitaker, Lou, 148
White, Frank, 75
Wilkinson, J.L., 73
Williams, Dick, 135
Williams, Mitch "Wild Thing," 123
Williams, Ted, 76, 133, 135
Wilson, Hack, 95
Wilson, Jimmie, 115
Wooden, John, 118
Worrell, Todd, 78
Wrigley Field, 98, 136, 138–143
    also see "Friendly Confines"
Wrigley, Phillip K., 142–143
Wrigley, William, Jr., 139
"Wrigleyville," 139
Yankee Stadium, 31, 51, 150–155
    also see "The House That Ruth
    Built"
Yastrzemski, Carl, 133, 135
Yawkey, Thomas A., 133, 134
Yom Kippur, 43

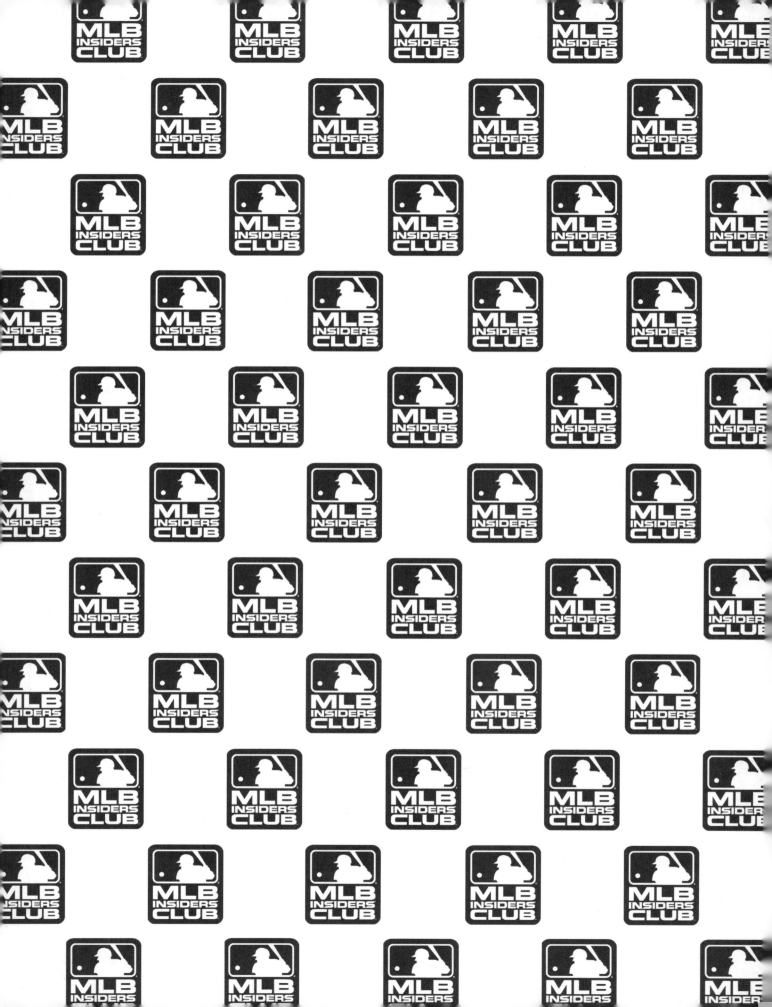